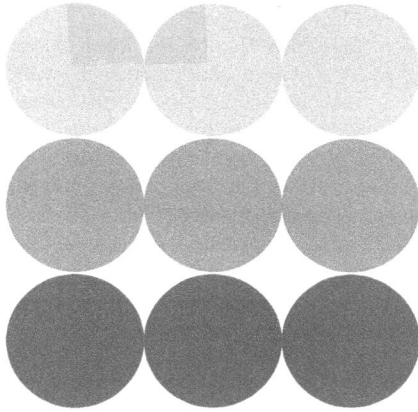

Profitable Routines

Create a Winning Sales Plan
to Grow your Business

CHRISTOPHER BATES

Printed in the United States of America.

Profitable Routines: Create a winning sales plan to grow your business.

Library of Congress Control Number: 2013932401

ISBN 978-0-9889360-0-3

Table of Contents

Introduction • 1

Part One: The Sales Maturity Model • 9

Part Two: Craft Your Sales Plan • 47

Part Three: Adopt, Adapt, and Accelerate • 101

Acknowledgments • 135

About the Author • 137

Workshops and Training • 139

Index • 141

Introduction

Not long ago, a global financial services company asked my consulting firm for help. The economy had taken a nosedive, and their investors were no longer investing. For twenty-five years, this company had thrived on word of mouth advertising. Because their investment products were so lucrative, almost selling themselves, the staff and management had settled into a "windfall" sales culture.

But in the preceding nine months, sales had dropped fifty percent. This was unprecedented in company history. This sales team was well-trained, professional, and experienced. They knew every tactic in the book. Sales performance had never been a problem. So this sudden sharp decline had the management team's full attention, and they were deeply concerned.

"It doesn't make sense," one vice president told me. "We have the highest rates of return on the most secure products available in this crazy up-and-down market. This is the very time people should invest in our products. We have a track record that proves we know how to navigate these economic storms."

When we discussed the strategic differences between a "windfall" market, a "hunter" market, and a "farmer" market (we will define these terms in the next section), their executives recognized some fundamental flaws in their current approach to sales and marketing. In short, their strategy had fallen out of step with their target market—so their target market had stopped responding. Even the best efforts of their best sales people were now out of sync with the needs and expectations of their best prospects.

Their best sales efforts by their best sales people were no longer aligned with the needs and expectations of their best prospects.

Fortunately, when they became aware of the misalignment, this leadership team did not turn militant, accusing each other and laying (or avoiding) blame. They had the wisdom and maturity to depersonalize the problem. So, instead of turning against each other, they shared the problem and the resolution. These leaders cooperated over the next few weeks, and plotted how best to shift their team's strategies from "windfall" to "hunter," and how to adapt their organization to provide more support for those sales reps already functioning as "farmers."

We worked with management to identify their high, mid, and low sales performers, and designed a reliable selling system for each group. Then, we used the simple concepts found in Profitable Routines to design new processes and training to allow each account manager to plan and execute a rock-solid sales strategy and rebuild a book of business. Finally, we adapted their sales tracking software to support this new focus with better automation and simplified activity and opportunity management.

A few weeks later, we presented this new system to the sales teams in a series of face-to-face, on-site training events nationwide. Once the sales reps sensed the commitment and effort their management team had given to address these issues, and understood the root cause of company's sales performance problems, the staff became receptive to the new plans. They came to understand that their sales had dropped because their market had shifted, and that they must adjust to win. As we discussed these new strategies, tactics, and methods, they said they felt more in control and had a much clearer vision of how they could realistically meet their sales goals month after month. More clarity, in fact, than they had ever had before.

Those hopes were realized. Within ninety days, the team once again filled their company's sales pipeline with real opportunities. Within nine months, their sales revenues grew by double digits.

Same company. Same leadership. Same products. New sales strategy. That is the power of a team that is aligned with their target market and executing Profitable Routines.

A clear approach to sales strategy

As sales professionals, it is our responsibility to shift and change as our marketplace shifts and changes, to stay relevant and engaged. But over time, we inevitably fall out of sync with our target market. Sometimes, we fall into self-imposed traps that limit our sales performance. In other cases, management directives emphasize outdated tactics, denying us the flexibility and creativity required to adjust to our target market. Eventually, sales performance falters.

But knowing we are out of touch is not enough. A patient may know they are sick, but not know why. They need a diagnosis before they can begin treatment. So, how do we diagnose the root cause of our poor sales performance? For example, what needs to change when our old way of prospecting is no longer filling the sales pipeline? Or when our lead conversion rate drops?

When sales performance drops, it is an instant company crisis. Without a clear framework to accurately diagnose and address these problems, we find ourselves under increasing pressure to perform, with fewer tools to succeed, forced to follow sales strategies that are driven by blind panic rather than methodical planning and market intelligence.

Here are five ineffective strategies often employed by a struggling sales team:

- ∞ **The Shotgun Approach**—Inconsistent or "scattered" sales efforts, with no clear definition of their target market, no segmentation, no prioritization, no rhyme nor reason to their prospecting. Without a methodical system to guide their efforts, they cannot positively measure, manage, and direct those efforts, know who to talk to next, or what they want or need.

- ∞ **The Bulldog Approach**—Focused, to a fault, on just one thing at a time. One particular channel, lead source, or market segment dominates the majority of their sales efforts. These teams waste time and energy as they just keep doing what they have always done, without periodically assessing their position in the marketplace. Their hyper-focus on a limited set of tactics, strategies, products, or prospects causes them to ignore valuable "low hanging fruit" right in front of them.

- ∞ **The Come-to-Me Approach**—All language, communications, and presentations are focused on this team's own needs, *their* sales process, *their* products, *their* plans, *their* culture, *their* company, *their* goals… rather than demonstrating they understand and care about what their prospects care about. They miss important opportunities to build long-term relationships for repeat business.

- ∞ **The Bright Shiny Objects Approach**—Enamored with fads, tricks, and gimmicks, some sales teams are constantly looking for short cuts to win deals. Some fads are innocent and beneficial in that they keep us open, learning, adapting, and probably best of all: motivated and moving. But gimmicks lack the staying power and reliability of a selling system that works, besides burning out great sales teams, and worse—making prospects suspicious.

- ∞ **The Numbers Game Approach**—Some teams count raw numbers of phone calls, emails, presentations, demos, and onsite visits, staying busy instead of focusing on qualified sales leads, high probability deals, areas of proven performance, and the number of deals closed each week. Simply measuring numbers rewards those who make a hundred calls a week to Low-Value unlikely buyers, and punishes team members who make ten calls a week to High-Value, likely buyers.

If you or your sales team have faced any of these challenges, Profitable Routines can help.

What you will find in this book

I hope you picked up this book because:

- ∞ It is incumbent upon you to sell

- ∞ You don't want gimmicks - you love real, solid plans

- ∞ You feel your product/market/service still has vast, untapped potential

- ∞ You have been successful in sales, but what worked before is no longer working, and you're not sure what changed

- ∞ You are ready to be inspired

- ∞ You don't mind working hard, making calls, and doing the things it takes to make a sale

Imagine you have been asked to create a plan to introduce a new product to a new target market, or to promote a new service offering to your existing customers. If you execute your new sales strategy well, it could result in a huge business breakthrough for your company; but if you fail, you may find yourself looking for work. How can you create a sales and marketing plan that has the highest potential for success, a plan specifically tailored to your target market, to your Ideal Buyers' needs and language, and to your sales team's true capacity to execute?

Thousands of sales professionals worldwide have validated the Profitable Routines sales plan. It is the culmination of more than 10,000 billable consulting hours spent side-by-side with some of the most effective salespeople in the world, sales teams large and small, across a breadth of industries and organizations. It is what the "best of the best" do every day, almost without thinking—like second nature—and represents regular habits or patterns that lead to success. These principles have turned entire companies around, opening the floodgates for revenue from new and former customers, and allowing them to set aside unproductive and "flavor-of-the-week" sales tactics.

The first concept we will introduce is the Sales Maturity Model. The Sales Maturity Model will teach you to recognize, articulate, and selectively employ three basic sales strategies. Just as poor posture creates stress in our bodies, poor alignment between our sales efforts and the needs and expectations of our target market will create unnecessary stress and tension in the sales environment. The Sales Maturity Model is all about positioning your team's efforts to maximize their impact and give you the best shot at success.

Next, we will examine the Profitable Routines sales plan in detail, including the five essential disciplines of any winning sales plan. These five activities will help you quickly find untapped potential in your target market, and design a system or method with a set of routines or action plans that will focus your team on capturing that business.

Finally, in the last section of this book, we will walk through the implementation of Profitable Routines step by step, to help you create your new sales strategy and prepare for rapid, scalable business growth. I understand that few of us have time to stop what we are doing (selling) for several weeks to work through the Profitable Routines sales plan. So this last section of the book is designed to help you adopt this new method one step at a time, while delivering immediate results and a net gain in sales focus every time you complete a section.

I have had the pleasure of interacting with some of the best and brightest in sales and marketing today: global business leaders, mid-market corporate executives, and smart, savvy bootstrapping entrepreneurs. What has emerged from these team efforts to improve sales effectiveness is a common framework that supports steady revenue growth in any industry, with any product—a framework that recognizes the limitations and nuances of human performance, different styles, and unique personalities. I have used these tools and techniques to partner with thousands of business leaders, and have seen revenues grow and profits increase as a result.

Profitable Routines is that common framework. It is a set of principles that will allow any company, in any market, in any economy, to flex, adapt, and refocus their sales efforts into a strategy that makes sense for that very moment. These principles are tried and true, and should be part of every sales professional's playbook. They are simple, they work, and they are some of the basic building blocks of any growing business.

Assuming your product or service resonates with your target market and you can focus on these fundamentals long enough to see results, I am confident that Profitable Routines will help you create a sales strategy to maximize your efforts and generate growth for you and your company.

Part
One

The Sales Maturity Model

1

The Power of Alignment

More than any other single dynamic—more than the product you sell, your branding, your years of experience, your training, your boss, your personality or style—the greatest predictor of your success in sales is how well you understand your Ideal Buyer. The needs and desires, preferences and affinities, people and budgets within your sales territory are the raw materials of your achievement. We cannot commit ourselves to a sales strategy until we first commit ourselves to our target market, then discover how best to serve them.

As sales leaders, we are entrusted with the care and well-being of this segment of the global marketplace that we call "home." From this territory, we derive a sense of our professional identity, and we earn our keep. Our calling is to nurture, shepherd, steward, and invest in this territory whose roads we drive, whose children we know, whose language we speak, and whose worldview we share.

Your target market is the environment in which everything you do to make a sale has to make sense. Your Ideal Buyers—those people you would most love to engage within your target market—predetermine the direction and success of your sales strategy. They dictate the expertise, conviction, commitments, and actions necessary for you to grow your book of business. Historians have a proverb: "Geography is destiny." In sales, your Ideal Buyer shapes your strategy. Long-term success in sales requires that you serve this community well, that you become recognized as a thought leader, as the hub of a relational network, enriching it, and helping it thrive.

●●●

If you are a native of your 'territory', then you naturally and easily understand your Ideal Buyer's culture, their concerns, and their needs. If you are a recent immigrant to that territory, however, you must learn those things as a second culture.

●●●

The basis for your excellence in sales is how well you understand and invest in this ecosystem that is your target market. Your Ideal Buyer can sense whether you are truly committed to their cause, to their tribe, to their point of view, or whether you have borrowed your conviction from someone else, leased it as a mercenary who is loyal only temporarily, or only to yourself. But you will never hit your stride in sales if you do not understand your Ideal Buyers, if you do not truly care for them as a group, if you are not deeply committed to each of them. Trust is not easy credit—it is hard-won equity. Without that, you will never tap the passion that makes people buy based on the conviction in your voice and their trust in your alignment with their goals.

If you are a native of your "territory," you easily understand your Ideal Buyer's culture, concerns, and needs. They are natural to you. If you are a recent immigrant to that territory, however, you must learn those things as a second culture. You carry, unknowingly, certain points of view and assumptions from your native land that your target market may not share. So in order to make sense to them, you need to adapt. In order to help your target market, you must enter into their world, understand their struggles, and compassionately but persuasively show them a better way.

Selling is not about your product, it is about their need. It is not about your pursuit plan, it is about their uncertainty. It is not about your quota, your promotion, or your incentive; it is about your Ideal Buyer's concerns, their desires, and the gap between where they are and where they want to be.

Introducing the Sales Maturity Model

But, here is the challenge: your target market is never static. It is always changing, shifting, and adapting around you. These changes are natural developments that follow a predictable pattern. As your "territory" matures along the Sales Maturity Model, your strategy must continually adjust to serve those companies and individuals effectively, and to capitalize on the business transactions taking place within that target market. Your sales environment, dictated by your target market, contains variables that can impact your sales performance for better or worse. Each stage of this continuum—Windfall, Hunter, and Farmer—requires a unique language and approach to capture the untapped potential in that market, at that moment. You could design the perfect sales plan for your product, but if your strategy does not match the market's expectations—you will fail. In the chapters that follow, we will further define explore deeper insights to help you thrive in each stage.

The Sales Maturity Model becomes painfully obvious when you fall out of alignment or out of sync with your target market. As your market shifts from Windfall to Hunter, for instance, your sales approach will lag a bit, creating a gap between your attitudes, terms, and expectations and those of your target market. Confusion can quickly set in as sales revenues drop sharply, and nothing seems to work anymore as you try frantically to adjust and adapt quickly to the new conditions. But those adjustments take time, and they should be approached methodically, not haphazardly.

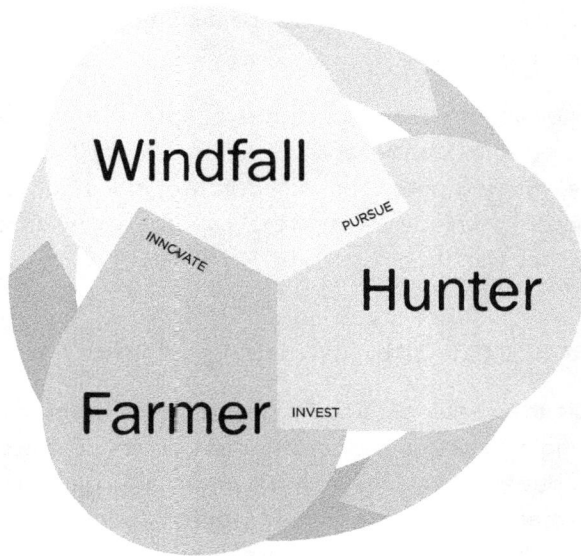

Figure 1—The Sales Maturity Model reflects the natural cycles of a marketplace

This is where many sales plans and strategies prove inadequate. Blindly trying new tactics overlooks the underlying cause of the drop in sales revenues. Grasping for gimmicks does not realign you with your target market. When the market shifts, you must first come to understand this new sales environment before you can redesign your selling system or plan to, once again, maximize every call, hour, and conversation. In truth, understanding your sales environment and staying aligned with your target market is just as critical to planning a new strategy as your day-to-day sales tactics and techniques.

Some sales reps may try to overcome these natural, seasonal market forces by sheer force of personality. They assume they can simply select a sales strategy that fits their mood, and impose it on their prospects. That approach is exhausting, often extracting a high cost from the sales rep in terms of discouragement or disillusionment. Relying on personality above sensitivity may bring some limited or temporary success, but two questions haunt this optimistic sales leader:

- ∞ Will there be enough success to keep you afloat while you use trial and error to test your new sales approach?

- ∞ How long will the untapped potential in your market continue to wait patiently, underserved and unnoticed by competitors, while you figure out whether your new sales strategy is working?

But, when you take the time to properly align your sales strategy with your target market, every hour and every effort will expand your business and increase revenue.

Natural Cycles in the Marketplace

The Sales Maturity Model is probably best understood and employed as an endless growth cycle, an organic, seasonal process of learning, growing, pursuing, investing, testing, harvesting, learning, and so on. This model recognizes the natural cycles of demand and consolidation in your marketplace, and can help you quickly realign your sales techniques to respond effectively to those changes. Understanding the signs and seasons in your marketplace is crucial to developing an effective sales strategy. You must fully embrace, even embody, the marketplace you serve, staying in tune with its causes and effects, conditions, and opinions. Only then can you act with confidence and certainty on the sales plans on which you stake your future.

As a business leader, you can decide when to refocus your sales and marketing strategy to capitalize on and respond to each change as your marketplace matures along the Sales Maturity Model: from Windfall to Hunter, from Hunter to Farmer, from Farmer back to Windfall. These stages are flexible and dynamic, and innovation drives that flexibility. For example, if you are in a market with firmly established boundaries and recognized Farmers, and your firm introduces an innovative product or technology breakthrough, you could instantly create a Windfall dynamic in the market. Ideally, as you develop your new product, your sales and marketing teams are preparing to capture the majority of the new market with a Windfall sales strategy, organizing to move as quickly as possible, to maximize the strategic impact of the market shift you're about to create.

If the economy is booming and you are offering a unique product with obvious benefits to a hungry market, you can do quite well in Windfall mode. It would be a waste of precious time to "Hunt" during Windfall; the focus should be on order efficiency. Simply advertise and wait for the phone to ring, take the orders, and rake in the cash. To capture market share during Windfall, hyper-focus on branding, lead generation through advertising, and efficient order-taking systems. Growth is inevitable.

Six months later, however, a competitor may release a new product with more and better features than yours, and a lower price. Now, your sales tactics that were so effective last month are quite suddenly and dramatically out of alignment with your marketplace. How should you respond?

When the phone stops ringing toward the end of a Windfall period, sales leaders intuitively shift into "hunt" mode, demanding better prospecting and follow-up from their sales team. At this point, a high-pressure sales environment can quickly turn hostile, especially if the team lacks a shared understanding of the shift itself, and a common language to discuss their new reality. I have watched many good sales teams move into conflict as their market shifted within the Sales Maturity Model simply because they lacked the tools and understanding to collectively recognize and respond to these natural ebbs and flows of the marketplace.

As the volume of orders dwindles towards the end of a season of Windfall, smart Hunters will search out their best customers' commonly trodden paths and select a few "big game" targets from among those

Windfall customers to move forward to the next stage. Throughout the Windfall season, we must learn how our market thinks and behaves, so that we can later become Hunters. Rather than waiting for the phone to ring, Hunters learn the best way to select and pursue the best prospects. Thus, they develop an entirely new set of sales skills, tailored to their target market at a given point in time, and they begin to work much harder to win each deal than they needed to during Windfall.

As we learn what our target market wants, needs, and expects during the Hunter stage, those skills become instinctive. An experienced Hunter makes taking wild game look as easy as stalking a farm animal. As the market continues to develop through the Hunter stage, skilled and seasoned Hunters may decide to corner a certain type of game, perhaps stake a claim in a certain territory, and begin to invest in those selected smaller markets in order to become Farmers. To make the shift from Hunters to Farmers, we must learn how to select and steward long-term profitable relationships wisely. To become Farmers, we learn how to pick a good field, invest in that territory wisely, and stick around long enough to reap the rewards.

It is possible to proactively chart a course across the Sales Maturity Model, driving your organization to the front of the 'pack' and establishing your credentials as a true thought leader within your territory.

The sales reps we most love and admire make sales look effortless. In fact, an experienced Farmer makes every sale look like a windfall sale. They have gained credibility and earned trust in the marketplace. In truth, these professionals have carefully and consistently invested themselves as stewards of a given book of business, and what looks easy is in fact the fruit of their persistent labor, harvest after harvest, season after season. We recognize these Farmers as stoic leaders in our community. If, as a Farmer, you steward your territory well, then with harvest comes a true season of Windfall once again, and the whole lifecycle repeats. Only now, you are a year wiser and more experienced, and you are recognized in the community.

Established Farmers may employ strategic mergers and acquisitions to enlarge their territory, and thus their harvests. They may introduce discontinuous innovations (new products that render other products in the marketplace obsolete) in order to deliberately create new Windfall conditions in the market. These strategies undercut competitors, and capitalize on the massive attention created by huge, sudden volumes of transactions. This naturally increases the popularity of their brand, consolidates gains, and improves their recognition in the marketplace, further securing their territory and ensuring future harvests.

The key to leveraging the Sales Maturity Model to drive your sales strategies is two-fold. First, you must learn to recognize the telltale signs of each season, so that you can quickly settle on the new language, goals, objectives, strategies, and tactics that will align your behavior with the new thoughts and needs of your target market. Second, you as a true leader must find ways to influence your marketplace, so you are not simply reacting to the developments around you, but rather precipitating, catalyzing, leading, and influencing those changes. Develop a much stronger strategic advantage by plotting a deliberate course across the Sales Maturity Model, driving your organization to the front of the "pack," and establishing your credentials as a true thought leader within your territory.

The next few chapters examine the nuances, symptoms, needs, and strategies best employed to serve a market at each stage in the Sales Maturity Model.

2

> "No one can build his security
> upon the nobleness of another person."
>
> Willa Cather, *Alexander's Bridge*

The Windfall Sales Strategy

A Windfall sales strategy is reactive and efficient. The hallmark of a Windfall sales strategy is the stance of the sales team: they simply wait for the phone to ring. Often, sales revenues are only limited by transactional efficiency, or your ability to meet demand. It works well in bull markets, when buyers are knocking down your door and want your product yesterday. In Windfall, the marketplace is responding to your marketing efforts, to the pitch you made in your mass advertising. Your product or service is so compelling, and there is such a great need in the market, that the orders are literally rolling in almost faster than you can fill them.

Sales teams in Windfall mode support a high volume of transactions as efficiently as possible. Sometimes even a good team of actors or customer service reps could meet a Windfall quota, given the right technical product knowledge, because the market comes to you. That is the key—in Windfall, the buyer pursues the seller.

Windfall is ideal when:

- ∞ You are introducing a new product or service, especially if it represents discontinuous innovation (something so great, your prospects will change their behavior to get it)

- ∞ Your product practically sells itself

- ∞ Advertising and marketing, not sales, bear the brunt of lead generation and qualification

- ∞ The market is educated and demand is so high that buyers are already convinced and motivated to purchase

Word-of-mouth referrals are the golden key to Windfall. Referrals allow you establish recognition in a marketplace that is already looking for a provider. Referrals are the ultimate measure of customer satisfaction. They garner attention and trust that are rare and valuable in a retail or Windfall marketplace.

But even after orders have slowed or altogether stopped, many sales teams continue to function as if the market were still responding to a Windfall sales strategy. It is easy for sales to blame marketing or management for a sudden and unforeseen drop in revenues. In reality, your team must recognize that this is not a temporary problem—buyers and many competitors in the marketplace have already shifted and your team is now out of step. It is time to move on to the next stage in the maturity model.

Recognizing Windfall

For most teams selling to a Windfall market, sales revenues and growth statistics cannot be directly attributed to sales efforts. The concept with Windfall is that "all ships rise with the tide."

Since you are reliant on outside efforts for business development, and often have no control over the source and quality of your leads, actual sales performance is unrehearsed and inconsistent. Companies use Windfall to capture market share *en masse*, rather than to win individuals as advocates and evangelists for their product or brand.

The reactive nature of Windfall limits your sales capacity to the number of orders each sales rep can take in a day. This often creates end-of-month quota crises for most sales reps on a Windfall team. If management uses quotas as a "stick" type of incentive to keep staff on task, they will consistently set the quota just slightly out of reach every month. You may try up-selling and cross-selling techniques to increase revenue-per-sale, but the best strategy for growth in Windfall mode will include faster, streamlined automation to process more orders in less time.

Training for sales teams in Windfall mode focuses on product knowledge and efficient order processing. Some training may emphasize a certain attitude or style to ensure good customer service throughout the transaction. Gimmicks are often used either as promotions or as a way to exert control or influence over the buyer to get them to sign on the dotted line.

A unique blend of wisdom, caution, and decisiveness are required to know when to cut capacity once demand lags. Smart sales leaders will be ahead of this downward trend, and will already have a Hunter strategy prepared and ready for training and execution.

Hiring new sales reps for a Windfall team is not normally a problem. A team of professional-sounding, low-cost employees can be trained to follow a script convincingly. Investments to support a Windfall sales strategy are often far greater in marketing and advertising than in compensating sales reps.

A fundamental flaw of the Windfall market is its unknown potential. Nobody is ever quite sure how many products the market will consume. Thus, planning for account acquisition is done at a macro level, rather than customer-by-customer. Contrast this with a Farmer strategy, in which the ultimate winner has carefully selected, courted, and won specific clients for their book of business. Thus, business planning and demands on the supply chain during a Windfall period can become serious challenges if sales results differ from projections.

In Windfall, you rely heavily on business development efforts to fill the top end of your funnel. You likely lack either the time or the interest to pursue a larger book of business, simply because that's not the best use of your energies—to "hunt" at this point would allow transactions to fall through the cracks.

Any business can employ a Windfall sales strategy effectively, and capture significant market share and recognition as a player in that market. Real estate, insurance, hospitality, retail, and most B2C (business-to-consumer) companies rely on Windfall as their de facto sales strategy. Those same companies that also employ a Hunter strategy will eventually put their competition out of business.

To Win at Windfall

The purpose of Windfall is to allow you to quickly capture market share, which requires that you convert attention to intention, and intention to transaction, as reliably as possible. The primary risk of windfall is that you will miss the signals that the market is shifting to the next level (Hunter).

Windfall works well in support of frenetic new market activity, such as a new product introduction, in which a marketing blitz is generating new interest that must be captured as sales. During a Windfall tornado when the phones are ringing off the hook, leaders should focus on daily execution, capacity, and tactics above strategy.

A sales team in a sustained Windfall market will naturally atrophy, becoming detached and reactive. A unique blend of wisdom, caution, and decisiveness are required to know when to cut capacity once demand lags. Smart sales leaders will be ahead of this downward trend, and will already have a Hunter strategy prepared and ready for training and execution.

To capitalize on a Windfall market, most leaders focus on a few key objectives:

- ∞ **Create** compelling products and services that resonate so strongly with the marketplace, their very existence generates demand

- ∞ **Perpetuate** that demand by delivering on expectations. Satiate the market's thirst. Keep your promises to build momentum and recognition in the marketplace

- ∞ **Consolidate** your gains by converting certain buyers into long-term relationships (Hunting), which will become the foundation for your longer-term business viability as the market moves into Farming conditions

How to Move Up

When the phone stops ringing, the Windfall strategy stops working. It is vital to shift quickly into a well-planned Hunter or Farmer strategy in order to consolidate your new market gains earned during the market's Windfall phase.

Focus on turning a transaction into a relationship through immediate tactics, such as follow-up for repeat business, up-selling, cross-selling, asking for referrals, and introducing product updates or service offerings to new product owners. Test the true loyalty of your customers by engaging them one-on-one in conversation, eliciting honest feedback about their buying experience.

For a deeper strategy, periodically review lists of new customers to identify potential new business partners that have appeared during fast-paced Windfall activity. Invest wisely in building relationships with those qualified, High-Value partners, and dive deep into those partner accounts with exclusive, win/win agreements. Leaders protect their time from unprofitable customers, carefully prioritizing by investing in relationships with a longer lifespan than a single transaction.

Lastly, engage your entire team in a "lessons learned" session to refine and improve your process. Discuss advertising, marketing, lead generation, business development, and qualification systems, and define some action steps based on what you have learned about your target market's preferences and expectations.

Self-Assessment: Are you in a Windfall market?

Answer the following questions with a simple "yes" or "no."

_____ Is the current demand for your products or services primarily driven by a "new and improved" dynamic? By innovation? By the latest research and development?

_____ Are your sales efforts primarily reactive (responding to inbound communications from prospects) rather than proactive (chasing down prospects with follow-up calls)?

_____ Is your sales process fast and efficient, primarily focused on taking the customer's order rather than influencing or persuading the customer?

_____ If you had to train someone to do your job, would your sales training focus on product knowledge and how to complete the paperwork for the order, rather than prospecting, qualifying, or pursuing sales opportunities?

Next, we'll examine the dynamics of a Hunter sales strategy, then move on to study the Farmer marketplace. At the end of this section of the book, we will review your responses to the questions above.

3

> "Many of our fears are tissue paper thin,
> and a single courageous step would
> carry us clear through them."
>
> Brendan Francis Behan

The Hunter Sales Strategy

A Hunter strategy is account acquisition and order pursuit at its most aggressive. When the phone stops ringing towards the end of a Windfall period, sales managers rightfully demand their team quickly become Hunters. The big game deals are no longer just walking right into your sales funnel, lured by your attractive bait. Your target is now more wary, more cautious, and less hungry.

A Hunter market is not a place for the faint of heart. It welcomes the new and immature, but will only support aggressive, proactive prospecting. Sales capacity is often limited by your force of personality and the number of hours in a day. To the untrained eye, a good Hunter may appear to be "dating" their prospects. Hunter is an ideal growth stage for transitional or stagnating markets. But eventually, Hunters who do not learn to become Farmers must learn to live with hunger.

The Hunter strategy is highly dependent on the personality of each sales rep, and is often heavy-handed in its tactics. There are a lot of leads to pursue in a short amount of time, so the immediate transaction is more important than the long-term relationship. A Hunter is proactive and aggressive. A Hunter strategy requires that you get good at locating and targeting game. Good Hunters find out where their target market hangs out, and learns make sense to that market, rather than alarming them or scaring them off. Good Hunters learn to be subtle, attractive and practical in order to find and capture new business.

Recognizing Hunter

Unlike Windfall, and far more than Farmer, a Hunter strategy is proactive and highly tactical. It requires an approach that is uniquely designed for the Hunter's specific territory, industry and customer base. The focus is on quick and easy wins that will help consolidate the gains made during Windfall.

A Hunter strategy is ideal when:

∞ Your book of business is undefined or still developing

∞ Sales training is focused on prospecting and closing skills

∞ Sales hiring is focused on sales personalities and aggressive prospectors or closers

∞ Sales performance is driven by hunger or outside pressure

∞ The market potential for your product or service is still largely untapped

∞ Your market itself is immature and untested (by both you and your competitors)

To Hunt Well

During a Hunter market, success comes from diligent focus on a few strategic objectives:

- ∞ **Prospect** methodically based on intelligent decisions in customer segmentation, prioritization, and messaging

- ∞ **Pursue** untapped potential diligently in your target market, including buyers and partners

- ∞ **Profit** on every deal, politely declining any that will not carry its own weight in terms of cost and profit margin

Successful Hunters have a unique capacity to sustain high energy yet still remain sensitive to prospects. They have disproven the theory of the numbers game, and instead intuitively woo and close deals with buyers who have seemingly disparate needs. They are neither fancy nor deep, but rather focus on sales fundamentals, constantly evaluating and improving their ability to make presentations, answer objections, and consistently follow up with prospects.

Successful Hunters do not avoid the daily grind of sales. They are internally motivated risk takers who crave unlimited earnings potential, so if your compensation plan does not support their ideas of risks and rewards or their aggressive career goals, they may very well lose interest and move on.

A gimmick-of-the-week approach may provide Hunters with some immediate revenue, but short-lived mind tricks eventually demoralize your best sales reps, and confuse analysis of strategic decisions by magnifying inconsistent results. Mature Hunters never focus exclusively on a single "Big Play" or the "Biggest Deal of All".

Most Hunters could become more productive with stricter lead qualification, to help them invest in sales pursuits that are more likely to pay off. Support them in nailing down a simple sales process, including three or four early qualifying questions, and you can improve their performance almost overnight.

For new or inexperienced Hunters, it is crucial to develop profitable daily and weekly routines that cover all the basics of prospecting, follow-up, and a next step to move each deal forward through the sales pipeline.

How to Move Up

Some Hunters actually love the game of sales so much that they have no desire to settle down with a book of business and become a Farmer. Of course, it is important to develop a sales strategy that will keep your team motivated and performing at their best, so be aware that some sales professionals may be happier living for years in a Hunter strategy. Don't hold them back. As long as your target market will support Hunters, and they are properly incentivized, these sales reps will help you continue to grow your market share while others consolidate gains and focus on nurturing and retaining their book of business with a Farmer strategy.

Ideally, a Hunter strategy should always be moving towards Farmer, simply because this is the natural progression of any target market. To do this, it is important to periodically review and rank each account for untapped potential. Carefully watch where your team is gaining traction and attention in the marketplace. Eventually, an emerging market will appear where your team has recognized ability and delivers results. Gather customer stories and reference accounts to land three to five anchor accounts as big fish for your book of business. Then, leverage those relationships to build a solid, stable brand and establish your company as a major player in the market.

The timing of your move from Hunter to Farmer is critical. You cannot impose a Farmer strategy on your target market simply because you are a tired and hungry Hunter. While the line between a Windfall market and a Hunter market is often clear and quickly drawn, the shift from Hunter to Farmer is rarely so. More often, Hunters are shocked when they suddenly begin to run into fences as they stalk big game, those "fences" being the territory staked out by competitors.

Ultimately, your success as a Farmer depends heavily on the strength, skill, and tireless, deliberate efforts that helped you succeed as a Hunter. The best Hunters become Farmers not when they are tired of hunting, but when their best prospects are tired of being hunted, and are ready to settle down with a long-term business partner. The herd recognizes their caretaker, and responds, "You know us. You have our best interests in mind. You can shepherd and steward us well. Please settle down and we will join you."

Self-Assessment: Does Your Market Expect to See Hunters?

Answer the following questions with a simple "yes" or "no."

_____ Does your sales performance depend heavily on proactive prospecting and pursuit of sales opportunities?

_____ Are your attitude and relational skills just as important (or sometimes more important) to closing deals as the features and benefits of your product or service?

_____ Does your ideal prospect expect you to approach them with a product, a plan, and a proposal, assuming you will guide them through a sales process before they buy?

_____ Would your sales performance immediately benefit from having a higher volume of new leads, a more selective set of lead qualification criteria, or both?

4

The Farmer Sales Strategy

One autumn, a young city boy escaped Urbana to clear his mind with a drive through the country. A few hours after the city's concrete canyons ejected him from smoke and smog, he found himself on a dusty two-lane road, winding between hills and creeks. Nestled deep in every third or fourth valley was a small town, conveniently labeled with a water tower. In between, homes were kept safely distant by fields rich with crops, and orchards heavy with harvest.

His car finally rolled to a slow stop alongside one such orchard. An old farmer stood among his apple trees, examining the crop as workers around him filled baskets, tractors, and warehouses with shiny red fruit.

"Wow! That is amazing!" said the young man. "You must have tons of apples here! These things are really expensive in the shops downtown. How long does it take you to grow a crop like that?"

The farmer turned slowly and eyed the boy's car, then his suit, and finally, his young face.

"'Bout sixty-seven years, son."

Farmer, the most mature sales strategy, requires total mastery of the skills used in the prior stages, but adds deeper thought leadership, a more mature strategy, and long-term, sustained effort. Farmers establish their territory. They learn it, take ownership of it, and steward it well, sowing and reaping season after season after season. They are always looking for more "good soil" to invest in, but expansion comes more thoughtfully and with a better-informed strategy.

●●●

Becoming a successful Farmer requires a deep, long-term commitment to, and identification with, your target market. To win, it is absolutely vital that you become a recognized subject matter expert in your field.

●●●

A Farmer strategy creates and relies on an established book of business. Farming is the most mature and relational strategy available, but is not easily attained. You, your company, and your products and services must become recognized and trusted in the marketplace. Success as a Farmer is won through consistent, persistent, wise investments in your target market. For maximum impact, however, a Farmer strategy must begin while the market is still responding well to Hunters, when sales are hot and business is booming with no signs of slowing down.

A solid Farmer sales strategy begins with a focus on nurturing account relationships for **growth by addition**. Then, it shifts midstream, leveraging their new recognition as a market leader, and accelerates to gain market share with **growth by multiplication**. These teams strategically and purposefully move an entire marketplace from Hunter to Farmer, and in the process make themselves truly rich. The reward for their sensitivity to seasons, soil, and seed helps them garner enough recognition to influence the market as a whole, knocking out the mid-tier competition and emerging as "King of the Hill" in that market.

Once new boundaries are established, whether artificially from the outside, or organically from within the market itself, the die is cast.

Your organization must shift with the changing market and adapt its sales strategy to remain competitive and control costs with a Farmer strategy.

Think about Apple vs. Microsoft, Android vs. iPhone, Toyota vs. Ford, Blu-ray vs. HD. Once a particular sales organization forces the maturation of a market, there is attrition through economics among service providers and product lines, so that in the end, only two or three major players remain. Buyers are then forced to select not only a product, but a supply chain and format that will influence many subsequent purchase decisions.

Occasionally, outside forces may force a market to mature rapidly, so that Hunter is no longer an adequate, appropriate, or efficient strategy. The earliest indication of this is the imposition of new boundary lines among buyers or competitors. Government regulations, geographic constraints, or new competitors (through mergers or acquisitions, for instance), or some other outside force may require us to recognize and adhere to these new boundaries.

Recognizing Farmer

Farmers identify, capture, and steward a profitable book of business. They leverage natural business cycles and seasons in the marketplace. They are not as focused on the immediate wins or short-term goals that Windfall and Hunter strategies require. Farmers are patient.

Farmer is the best possible sales strategy during a bear market, but it takes time, care, and deliberate investment to establish. Farmers build their empire on long-term relationships. The capacity of a Farmer is limited only to the marketplace itself, but they respect established competitive boundaries. Farmers are not just interested in a single transaction; their target market is looking for a long-term business partner or service provider who is recognized and respected in the community, and Farmers are happy to oblige.

A Farmer sales strategy is supported by proactive and strategic sales management. It is highly relational, and its reliance on a relational network can make it hard for outsiders to join or even understand the on-going dialogue.

Often, sales leaders with a Farmer strategy are seen as providing substantial thought leadership for the entire market. There is a focus on strategic development of new revenue streams, and a resistance to change that is often misunderstood, as it relies heavily on the status quo as a primary revenue source.

Training focuses on a holistic skillset for account acquisition and management. Hiring focuses on industry experience, networking, proven accomplishments, thought leadership, and the ability to build trusting relationships.

Sales efforts for Farmers are guided by long-term strategies and executed with daily discipline. Because the market for a Farmer is well defined, and boundaries well established, the potential for any new strategic initiative is measurable and most closely matches the whole market opportunity.

Good Farming

Becoming a successful Farmer requires a deep, long-term commitment to, and identification with, your target market. To win, it is absolutely vital that you become a recognized subject matter expert in your field.

In addition, in order to develop a mature book of business based on rich trust capital with clients, you must gauge when to work depth in the market, and when to work breadth.

For Farmers, effective leadership will ensure a fruitful harvest and promote steady growth. Common business objectives during this phase of the Sales Maturity Model suggest you:

- ∞ **Divest** or prune back your strategy by reducing efforts to sustain accounts that are no longer profitable

- ∞ **Invest** in new products or services that will win the hearts and minds of your current customers

- ∞ **Expand** your market share, both in depth (cross-selling and up-selling to existing buyers) and in breadth (growing the customer base with new accounts and partnerships)

Eventually, every Farmer reaches the realization that their ability to thrive in a mature marketplace is primarily limited by their own personal development. In order to become the leader your market deserves, you must grow, change, and adapt your behavior. Face your personal fears, and overcome them. Continue to sharpen your sales, presentation, and communication skills. Learn to develop win/win scenarios. Learn when to speak, and when to be silent. Learn when to act, when to wait, and when to push hard, uphill, for a long time, until you reap a harvest of new interest.

To control the "mental algae" of a slow-moving, contained market, stay abreast of all the latest news and research that is immediately relevant to your target market. Cast lines outside your industry to find new and compelling concepts that you can relate to the ongoing conversation in your community. In short, commit yourself to your target market as a distinct community for more than monetary purposes.

When to Shift Down

There are times when it's important, or even vital to survival, to downshift from a Farmer strategy to Hunter, or even back down to Windfall. Remember, this is about being sensitive and adaptable to market needs.

When industry changes threaten your customers' customers, alarms should sound within your sales organization. This is an early warning sign: your established territory may be at risk, and you should consider a new sales strategy. When your company adds new products or capabilities, and you have capacity to sell, it may make sense to preserve your current territory and engage a Hunter strategy alongside the Farmer strategy to both deepen and broaden your presence in the marketplace. When you lose several key accounts to new corporate policies, competitors, government regulations, or economic shifts, it may be time to return to a Hunter strategy to protect revenue sources.

Once, a Farmer Returned to Hunt

Successful Farmers begin as pioneers. They learn a new territory, build, invest, thrive, strategize, and work hard.

True humility, strength, and service to your marketplace will eventually require that you not only exhibit the ability to lead and be upwardly mobile, but also the humility, flexibility, and strength to once again become downwardly mobile.

Eventually, pioneers become settlers, and settlers work until they are satisfied. Satisfied Farmers begin to resist changes in the marketplace itself. They become the status quo all others must overcome in order to excel and stand out as remarkable.

It is difficult for an experienced, successful salesperson to downshift after living a comfortable life as a Farmer. You have achieved success, and arrived at a place of comfort—something you worked toward for years. Hunting now feels like a step backwards. It is more aggressive, more challenging, and while it is guaranteed you will get your hands dirty, the outcome of the hunt itself is uncertain. That uncertainty creates an embarrassing challenge to your self-confidence, which may not have been validated lately. Plus, the first time you downshift, moving from Farmer back to Hunter, it may feel like an admission of failure.

True humility, strength, and service to your marketplace will eventually require that you not only exhibit the ability to lead and be upwardly mobile, but also the humility, strength, and flexibility to become downwardly mobile. To return to Hunter, move out of the limelight, roll up your sleeves, and work once again without recognition or respect in the service of your community. Whether by drought, disaster, or design, every Farmer must eventually re-enter the ranks of the Hunters.

Mature Farmers neither neglect hard work, nor ignore reality. Markets shift and change rapidly, and what worked yesterday may not work tomorrow. Marketplace megacycles destroy the status quo on an irregular basis, requiring everyone to adapt, shift, and reinvent their circumstances. If you are committed to stand in the service of a given market, you will continue to do the hard work and open thinking required to lead, even if that means reminding other Farmers how to Hunt, and leading that charge by example.

Self-Assessment: Is Your Market Looking for a Farmer?

Answer the following questions with a simple "yes" or "no."

_____ Are the majority of your orders from repeat customers?

_____ Do you assume that most sales opportunities will include a comparison of your products and services to other major competitors?

_____ Could you take a two-week vacation without being concerned about meeting your sales goals or quota for that period?

_____ Are you as careful to pre-qualify prospects before entering into business with them as they are with you, so that you do not waste time on unprofitable relationships?

5

"Justifying a fault doubles it."

French proverb

Free Fall: The Un-Strategy

At least once in your career, you are likely to find yourself in a sales Free Fall without a safety net. Government regulations, economic downturns, announcements of litigation or scandal, natural disasters, and national emergencies create market forces that no one can predict, control, resist, or capitalize on.

Nobody in their right mind would choose Free Fall as a sales strategy. No single individual can initiate the mega-shifts that precipitate a Free Fall event. Free Fall is bigger than layoffs, budget cuts, your conflict with your boss, or losing That One Big Client. This is about major changes in the market that are way beyond your control. When the bottom falls out, everyone drops.

A well-trained, professional, opportunistic sales team can take advantage of almost any market condition except a Free Fall. With inventory to move, no buyers, and excess capacity, working harder may just prolong a losing proposition. But this is where every leader's true colors show, and character qualities like humility and honesty are of utmost importance.

When the bottom falls out of the market, your best possible strategy is to cut your losses early and preserve your relationships as best you can. Keep your promises, and tell the truth even when you cannot keep a promise. The discomfort of a lose/lose situation in business puts immense strain on relationships. If there is a silver lining to that cloud, it is this: when the economy recovers, you will know who you can trust, and so will your customers. Altruism, graciousness, and generosity reign supreme in these conditions. Refer your customers to your competitors. Give away excess product. Stay engaged in the conversation with your marketplace, heart-to-heart, and make every investment you can afford. Everyone will know who is committed to the market for the long haul by whether they build or burn bridges under duress.

You cannot anticipate or prepare a Free Fall strategy. Good businesses are built in spite of them and around Free Falls, not on them or because of them. In this situation, it is important to remember what will last, what will endure beyond the immediate crisis: your reputation, your character, and your relationships.

Free Fall is not a situation you would select. But you can choose a strategic, heartfelt response.

6

"One must wager on the future."

Elie Wiesel

To Everything, There is a Season

The Sales Maturity Model is a tool to help you quickly evaluate your sales environment, ensuring effectiveness in planning and executing sales for yourself, for a team member, or for your entire sales organization. The model recognizes that each of us works in a market that is plodding along at some level on the maturity continuum.

Your sales environment is fluid and dynamic, reflecting changes in your target market's needs and expectations. Often, these changes are driven by forces and dynamics outside your control, such as new product releases, innovation, overall market saturation, and technology adoption. Your response to those changes is critical and must be aligned with the instincts, needs, and expectations of your target market.

Each unique season in the Sales Maturity Model requires a distinct set of strategies, skills, training, and actions. Each season breeds signature tactics, attitudes, and dialogue among staff, management, and customers. And each has a proper time and place with strengths you can leverage under the right market conditions.

Used as a rapid assessment tool, the Sales Maturity Model will help you align and perfect your sales strategy with your target market. Used as a strategic planning tool, the model can serve as a guidebook, helping you recognize landmarks and plot your course as a trailblazer in your industry.

Once you have a clear understanding of how to align your sales strategy with your market using the Sales Maturity Model, you will have the perspective required to quickly identify breakdowns and bottlenecks in planning, execution, and leadership, and adjust your sales training, pursuit plans, and support systems to increase your team's effectiveness.

Geography is Destiny

Why did England rule the waves around the world for five hundred years? Historians tell us their geography both defined and enabled their strategy. The British developed shipbuilding and seafaring skills far earlier than surrounding cultures in order to support their commercial, political, and economic interests. With ports open year-round (the Norse were landlocked six months each year), the British were uniquely constrained and positioned to develop and employ strategies on the water. For five hundred years, their naval power extended around the globe.

Why did Mongols dominate northern China for centuries, expanding their territories, persistently taking new ground? How were they able to claim large tracts of land and successfully defend it from the prior owners? The grassy steppes of Mongolia required and supported the development of equine skills far superior to any other culture in the region. When the Mongols outgrew their own lands and expanded into northern China, their horses and riders were capable of surviving grueling conditions together. Their environment shaped their capabilities. The intimate trust, dependency, and unity that had developed between human and beast made the pair inseparable companions. Chinese warlords could not resist the power of the Mongol equestrians. Their conditioned skills gave them strategic and tactical advantages that granted them dominance in the region until gunpowder once again shifted the balance of power in the region.

Long before surrounding people groups, ancient Assyrians developed highly accurate mathematical calculations and the ability to navigate long distances over land and water based on astronomic observations. This was no coincidence. For generations, they had traveled across desert and sea without reference to landmarks. The Assyrians refined these critical skills and depended on them to support commerce and politics. Eventually, the Assyrian culture's advanced understanding of science, law, and civilization influenced more than half the globe for nearly a millennium, simply because their geographical territory dictated the development of new skills.

Your sales environment is fluid and dynamic, reflecting changes in your target market's needs and expectations. Your response to those changes is critical, and must be aligned with the instincts, needs, and expectations of your target market.

You work each day in a unique sales environment looking for leaders with skills, understanding, and ability to deliver a better way of life. The hopes, dreams, needs, and expectations of the "citizens" of your sales territory hold the keys to unlock the untapped potential of your success in sales.

Study your territory with patience, openness, and humility. Serve your territory with honesty, persistence, wisdom, and resilience.

Time to Pause and Reflect

Take a few minutes now to compare and study your responses to the self-assessments at the end of the Windfall, Hunter, and Farmer chapters of the book.

Which season or phase of the Sales Maturity Model do you believe is most closely aligned to your product or service, and your target market?

What words come to mind when you consider the dominant features of the "landscape" of your sales territory or target market?

What unique subtleties should influence your approach to prospecting for new leads, persuading buyers to purchase, and pursuing long-term business partners?

What are the most influential forces or dynamics shaping the psychology and direction of your target market today?

What kind of leadership is needed to drive your target market into its next stage within the Sales Maturity Model?

Who is most likely to assert that leadership?

Part Two

Craft Your Sales Plan

7

> "As to methods there may be a million
> and then some, but principles are few.
> The man who grasps principles can successfully
> select his own methods. The man who tries methods,
> ignoring principles, is sure to have trouble."

Ralph Waldo Emerson

Profitable Routines

There are two kinds of simplicity. First, standing innocently before us is the naïve simplicity of a child who has never negotiated conflicting ideas. Behind that untested child stands the battle-scarred warrior: trustworthy simplicity that has confronted complexity head on, slogged through it, and emerged on the other side, victorious. This strong, mature simplicity conquers exceptions and considers nuances, then looks back on us with a steady gaze and says, "What you are asking is hard work, but it is not complicated."

A naïve approach to sales strategy claims sales is a crapshoot. There are too many variables to guarantee anything. Sometimes you win, sometimes you lose. Are you feeling lucky today?

A mature approach to sales strategy recognizes that your sales plan must develop in full view of the complexities and nuances of your present-day marketplace. The Sales Maturity Model serves as a powerful framework for understanding those realities. Your plan must then be driven forward by tactics tailor-made to help more of your prospects buy more of your products. These are your Profitable

Routines—the specific tasks that will shape your efforts to profitably engage, grow, and expand your book of business.

In the first section, we explored the realities of your unique sales environment, contrasting the dynamics and nuances of Windfall, Hunter, and Farmer market conditions. Once you clearly understand how you can align your company, products, and sales and marketing efforts with your target market, you are prepared to move to the next stage in creating a sales plan to grow your business. In this section, we will examine the five key elements of a successful sales strategy. This is your selling system, which you can tailor and adjust to your sales environment at any time.

Like the rest of the universe, a sales strategy is based on certain natural principles that are neither complex nor negotiable. A farmer's crop or harvest is influenced by any number of variables: the health of the soil, the weather, the farming techniques used. In the same way, our sales efforts can be influenced by any number of variables—some of which we can control, others we can only respond to. If sales are suffering, the problem could be bad seed, bad soil, or weather. It may be the way you're farming the land or the problem could be your actual farming techniques: how you plant, nurture, grow, and harvest. In other words, given your seed, your soil, and your weather, what is the most effective strategy for getting a good crop this year? The selection and implementation of these techniques are the focus of this section, Profitable Routines.

What are Profitable Routines?

Establishing a set of "Profitable Routines"—a system for your regular work day or week—is key to helping you achieve sales goals. This is where preparation becomes performance, where big picture strategy meets day-to-day tactics.

The basics of selling haven't changed in years: build relationships, communicate well, make presentations, cultivate trust and rapport with prospects, drive to the close, employ good follow-up. All of those things are fundamental to selling. But without a strategy to employ them, mere fundamentals are no more effective than an ad hoc approach to sales and marketing.

The most successful sales teams I've met have several strategic elements in common. They have products that work, a dedicated sales team, a supportive management team serious about tried and true practices, and a sales plan that motivates and inspires the entire sales team through its sheer practical usefulness. Your sales plan must serve as the growth engine for your company. To be effective, it must win the trust of your entire team. It must be focused and immediately practical in order to generate immediate results. But it must also be flexible and open enough to accommodate individual personalities and market disparities among sales territories.

The Profitable Routines approach is not about planning every minute of every day, but rather focusing your best efforts, at this moment, on your most profitable actions, while leaving time to deliberately grow and develop new markets. These are the plays in your sales playbook, your personalized array of specific actions you need to take every day, every week, every month, to grow your book of business. Profitable Routines are also granular enough to support analysis, measurement, and continuous process improvement in future sales initiatives. This is business execution where the rubber meets the road, and strategy becomes both tactical and measurable.

There are five types of Profitable Routines. These are simple, repeatable disciplines. With these fundamentals in your playbook, no matter where you are in your day, your week, your psychology, or your emotions, you will always have something you can do to move your sales pipeline forward.

Here are the five types of Profitable Routines:

1. The Master List

2. Segment and Prioritize

3. An Ideal Buying Experience

4. Select and Pursue

5. Next Actions

In the next few chapters, we will explore each of these areas. There are many nuances to the Profitable Routines sales plan, particularly when applying these principles to various products, services, and industries. The next section focuses on the core concepts of Profitable Routines, and describes the system as simply as possible. In the final section of the book, you will have the opportunity to apply them to your specific sales environment, creating your own custom sales plan based on these principles.

8

"People who wait for a magic wand fail
to see that they are the magic wand."

Thomas Leonard

Routine #1: The Master List

Every effective marketing team I have ever worked with has excelled at three essential skills: clearly defining, segmenting, and prioritizing their target market.

That makes a lot of sense, if you think about it. Clearly defining your target market improves the focus of all your sales activities, because over time you get to know a lot more about your buyers' needs, frustrations, desires, personalities, and so on. The ideal sales scenario is this: to always have more untapped potential in your master list than you have time to pursue. This discipline helps you make the most of every moment you devote to selling.

Compiling a single master list of everyone you need to talk to in the coming months is a significant milestone for any sales strategy. And you don't just make this list once—you make the list, then routinely keep it up to date. I am continually surprised how few of the thousands of sales leaders I work with have listed all their known customers and prospects in one place. Even fewer have a set of regular routines in place to review, revise, and enhance these lists each month. Creating these lists of buyers and partners is a vital first step to creating a new sales plan.

One of my consulting clients is an adventure tour operator who sells all-inclusive, guided travel experiences for students. When I first began working with them they were a startup, and their sales team was eager to fill the trips they already had on the calendar. They were trying everything, shifting sales strategies almost weekly (a poor strategy in itself). But they could not seem to fill their sales funnel with more than a few legitimate opportunities.

We looked at their marketing strategy, which seemed sound.

We looked at their sales process, which was inefficient and required a lot of manual administrative paper shuffling. But until sales volume picked up, they could live with those inefficiencies.

When we looked at their definition of their target market (actually, their lack of definition), we found the real issue behind their lagging sales performance. Each sales rep was creating their own daily call lists using a "dart board" approach, arbitrarily searching the Internet for any school they could find within their territory that nobody had ever called. One sales rep would search for junior high schools in a suburb in Cleveland, pick up the phone, and cold call to try to reach anyone who might listen. Another would search for inner city charter high schools in Chicago, make the calls, and try to get someone on the phone who had lived outside the country or traveled internationally and might have interest in their travel packages. They were cold calling, into the blind, working hard and tracking sales notes and reporting their daily numbers to management. But there was no focus or strategy behind their pursuits, because there was no focus or strategy in their definition of their target market.

Until you know exactly who you are trying to reach and what they care about, sales is just a crapshoot.

So, we started asking questions to better understand their Ideal Buyer.

The first question we asked was, "Out of all the people you could pick up the phone and call right now, who has immediate buying power?" The answer revealed a market segment that would soon become our first selective focus: "Junior high and high school students, whose parents have the disposable income to pay the trip deposit today."

The second question was, "What is the fastest, easiest way to engage as many of these students as possible in their ideal buying experience?" The answer: "Leverage the teachers. Teachers know their students, and those teachers who have travelled internationally and value cultural exchange can promote us with school-wide assemblies, presentations, and events." Nice! We could establish those key relationships first, then leverage them to communicate with our target market (the students and their parents) en masse.

The third question was, "Which teachers are most likely to advocate your products and services?" The answer: "Teachers who travel regularly themselves during summer break. They value cultural exchange and international experiences, have stories to tell students, and would be good partners to join us on actual trips."

Based on that information, we popped open an Internet browser and searched for the top one hundred wealthiest zip codes in the country. It took less than ten seconds. We emailed that list to sales reps, and asked each to find the zip codes within their own territory. This, combined with a focus on a specific profile of a buyer, was their "target rich environment." Everyone understood that this was only a "phase one" sales strategy. But the new focus helped this ambitious sales team get traction in the marketplace right away, and filled their sales pipeline with immediate revenue relief. In the future, this team might cast their nets beyond this deliberately narrow focus to a broader and less exclusive market. But for now, we had to make sure they lived to see that day.

Next, each sales rep needed a list of schools to call. Some reps went directly to the Web to find the private schools in each of their zip codes, thinking this would further pre-qualify their prospects. Others looked up public or charter schools. Still others made no distinction. We allowed that variance for a reason: the sales reps were excited about this new focus. We had built it together, so they felt they owned it. And it created some healthy competition among the reps to see who could find the first "vein of gold." That competition generated speed and internal motivation, without pressure from management.

By the end of that afternoon, each sales rep had the names of three or four teachers who were passionate about international travel, and who influenced hundreds of students at schools where parents had disposable income.

With continued hard work and cold calling using this new list, my client's sales pipeline burgeoned. Within a week, trips were filling up with student enrollments and pre-trip deposits were rolling in.

This is not magic. There is nothing unique, special, or secret about this process. Clearly defining your Ideal Buyer empowers your sales reps. During a two-hour session together, we narrowed this sales team's target market from "any student in the country" (impractical to execute) to "teachers who travel internationally on a regular basis, at schools within the top one hundred wealthiest zip codes in the country" (a specific and measurable target). The results were immediate: better focus and productivity from the sales team, and positive responses from buyers and partners.

The Foundation of Your Sales Plan

Your target market is your entire universe of sales prospects in a single list. It includes buyers (individuals and organizations who will purchase your products and services) as well as partners (individuals and organizations who can help you market your products and services).

Here we come to our first Profitable Routine: creating and maintaining your "Master List" of buyers. This Master List will contain the names of people and organizations that fall into four categories:

- ∞ Current prospects
- ∞ Future prospects
- ∞ Current customers
- ∞ Former customers

Unless you are an undertaker, you probably hope for repeat business from most of your customers, In this context, I have included prospects, current and future, and customers, past and current, all under the universal term "buyer."

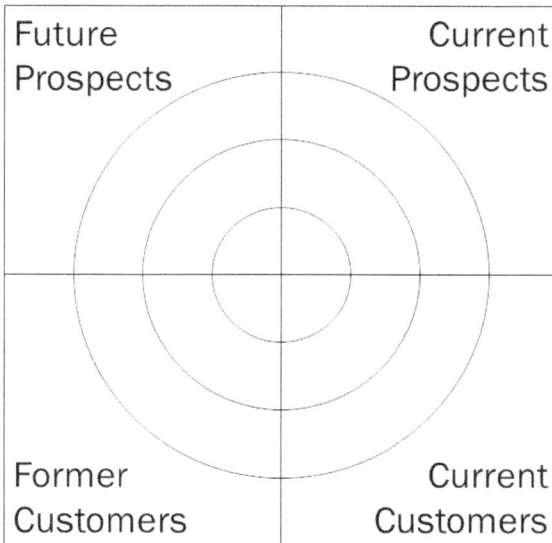

Figure 2—Four types of Buyers in your "Master List"

The first Profitable Routine is the process of listing all of your buyers and partners in one place—including those you already know, plus those you wish to engage. As you list these names, divide your "prospect universe" into targeted, segmented groups to be pursued as new or repeat customers.

Buyers and Partners

What is a "partner"? A partner could be a distributor or an agent, and is basically an outside representative not employed by you or your company who can help you sell products and services. With some partners, you might have a formal agreement includes a compensation plan. Or you might have informal relationships with individuals or organizations with whom you share leads and prospects because you have complementary products and are not direct competitors.

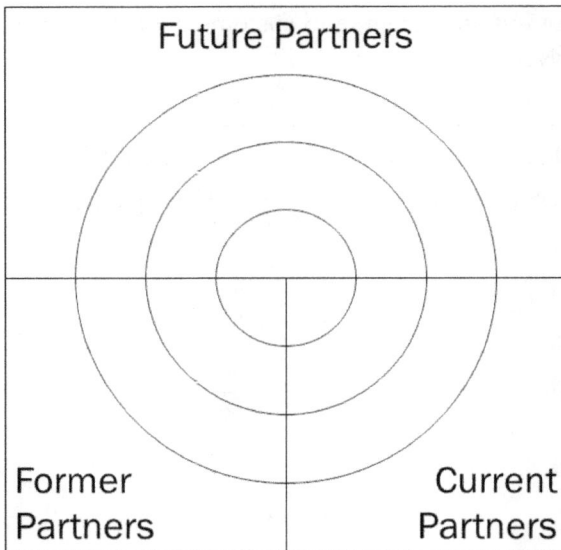

Figure 3—Your Master List of Partners

However you define them, a business partner is very different than a buyer. Some of your partners might play two roles: both buyer and partner - that's great! But these two personas are different enough in nature and in the way we engage them that we need to consider each separately. Both are vital to the success of your sales efforts.

We segmented our potential Buyers into four categories. But when we list Partners, we will initially group them into only three types:

∞   Current partners

∞   Future partners

∞   Former partners

As a rule, your Master List should always contain more business potential than you could close in the next calendar quarter. Most sales teams can list about a year's worth of potential business in their first pass with this exercise.

Opening the Floodgates

Creating and maintaining your Master List is an optimistic brainstorming exercise. This is the front end of your sales process. We will cover a new prioritization process in the next chapter, so you can be assured that any bad apples or ridiculous ideas will be culled out at that time. While you are brainstorming lists of names in your target market, it is important to just list as many names as you can. Here's how:

∞   Review lists of leads sent to you by your company or business partners

∞   Review lists of orders from last year, the prior year, even two or three years back

∞   Network with people who might know potential buyers or partners

∞   Ask for referrals from everyone, whether they buy from you or not

∞   Look through your social media contacts

∞   Consider purchasing lists from data clearinghouses

For instance, if you are working in an established business with a stable market, you might be thinking, "It's just not that easy. I can't pull new leads out of thin air!" Not every sales team enjoys an entrepreneurial green field opportunity. Some of you have worked for many years in the same industry, with the same products, even at the same company. For you, adding new names to your Master List might be a brief annual exercise, not a series of hourly epiphanies. If this is you, take heart. In working with thousands of sales leaders, many of whom have been in slow-moving, well-established markets, I have found that this first Profitable Routine (creating and maintaining a Master List) has opened the minds of even the most entrenched sales teams to new opportunities. Those opportunities may be further out and require more effort to achieve, but sometimes that is the market environment in which you must find a way to succeed.

> ●●●
> **For any sales team serious about growing revenues, creating and maintaining a Master List of buyers and partners is the first step toward an accurate, empathetic understanding of your target market. This is the "true north" compass heading that will lead you to your optimal sales strategy.**
> ●●●

What is the alternative? Status quo? My friend, if there is money to be made in your target market, and you are not doing the work to benefit from that untapped potential, rest assured that those prospects who truly need your products or services will beat a path to your competitor's doorstep. For an established business like yours, your best potential buyers may not lie among your Future Prospects, but among your Former Customers. Employee turnover within your customer base could prove to be a profitable vein of gold for you, but if you don't embrace a discipline of creating and maintaining a Master List, how would you ever know? Do not accept past failures as limits to your future success. Replace self-imposed, self-defeating limitations, such as thinking there are no new prospects within reach, with the understanding that you are here to build long-term relationships. Letting people know you are committed to your market is a worthy task, regardless of how likely they are to buy from you.

If you are just beginning to build a new book of business, regardless of where your market is in the Sales Maturity Model it is absolutely essential for you to learn and hone your prospecting skills, and that begins with your Master List. Without a cadre of existing customers and the stories and confidence that accompany an established clientele, the exercise of making lists, prioritizing, selecting, and pursuing the right buyers and partners will be the foundation on which you build success upon success, sale upon sale, and move steadily toward your goals.

For any sales team serious about growing revenues, creating and maintaining a Master List of buyers and partners is the first step toward an accurate, empathetic understanding of your target market. This is the "true north" compass heading that will lead you to your optimal sales strategy. The names on this list will guide your efforts over the next ninety days as you prove to yourself and your team that there is still immense untapped potential in your target market.

From a practical standpoint, your Master List should always be available to you as you go through each sales day. This list is the "core" of a Profitable Routines sales plan that is tailored to your unique goals, and allows you to maximize your productivity each week.

After you have created this "backlog" of sales calls, it is time to think strategically about the names and categories of prospects on this list. It is time to get into their hearts and minds and to understand their needs, desires, and goals. In the next chapters, we will segment and prioritize these names and create action plans to pursue the business potential in your Master List.

9

"Three rules of work:
Out of clutter, find simplicity;
from discord, find harmony;
in the middle of difficulty lies opportunity."

Albert Einstein

Routine #2: Segment and Prioritize

If you were only allowed three sales calls each day, and you had to make those calls really count to move you towards your sales goals, whom would you call? *More importantly, how would you decide whom to call?* That question captures the essence of segmenting and prioritizing your sales opportunities. As a sales professional, time is your most finite commodity. There are only twenty-four hours in a day, and only so many hours each day to see prospects. A wasted or unproductive prospecting hour is your worst enemy.

I worked with an investment firm a few years ago that had a well-established book of business, but felt it was time to expand by allowing independent agents to market and sell their products. They had focused on this effort for half a year, and had seen some good success, but their executive team felt they had not fully hit their stride in the new market. Something was holding them back, preventing them from achieving the growth trajectory they'd planned the year before.

We worked through the Profitable Routines process together, adapting it to their business context as we went. Along the way, we discovered that each of their representatives had their own unique way to identify, recruit, and work with these new investment brokers.

A few of the newer, younger reps were convinced they just needed to plow through hundreds of names and they'd find a few "rainmakers" in the process, agents who would bring them a flood of investors, allowing them to then sit back and coast. In truth, they were looking for a short cut—a way to achieve the lifestyle they observed in their most successful peers, but without doing the hard work of establishing their own fruitful book of business as a Hunter. So, these young sales reps would search desperately for any list they could find. They chased down lists of brokers that were not yet claimed by another rep, lists of brokers that just graduated from college, and lists of brokers that just moved into the area. They would start taking those brokers to lunch, coffee, beers, or a ball game, trying to schmooze their way into a partnership.

Some of the more detail-oriented reps tried to systemize the entire process with databases and spreadsheets, using complex scoring algorithms to try to determine which leads would be the best for them to pursue. They only called on the "cream of the crop", based on their criteria. The rest of the time, they obsessed with making sure every name on their lead list was properly capitalized, had an address, a phone number, the career history of the broker, the breed of their dog.

The most successful reps were the quietest. They simply went about their business, spending about half their time in the office, half in the field. They were seldom rushed or frantic, yet never wasted a moment of time. They were focused, clear, and confident.

Each of these sales reps seemed to have a good grasp on their target market of brokers to recruit as agents or business partners. Their lists were indeed current and well organized. They obviously had a great suite of products, profit margin, and proven performance to pitch to prospective agents. And their team was working hard each week to achieve activity targets for sales calls and follow-ups. What was missing from their strategy? Why were their efforts to sell profitable products to a hungry market through a new channel proving difficult?

The answer became evident when we began to discuss *how each sales rep prioritized their lists* of prospective agents, to determine which of those prospects were worth pursuing. For this sales team, a "High-Value" prospective agent already had an established book of business—a livery of investors who

❧❧❧

Two companies with identical products, but disparity in their understanding of their target market or the way they segment and prioritize leads, will execute totally unique sales strategies. Inevitably, one will outperform the other.

❧❧❧

were open to new opportunities. A "Low-Value" prospect was new to the game. A "Low-Effort" prospect was proactive, meaning once they understood my client's products and business, they would consistently bring my client face to face with theirs to make deals. A "High-Effort" agent was reactive—they never called my client's sales team, never introduced their clients. They seemed to need a baby sitter more than a business partner.

This simple but profound clarification made all the difference to this highly capable, experienced sales team. They immediately set to work prioritizing their lists of current and prospective agents based on these "Proactive vs. Reactive" and "Established vs. New" criteria. Results came quickly. In just over two months, they had nearly doubled the number of orders booked through third party agents, culled out ineffective agents, and recruited several new strategic partners.

Your new sales strategy is going to be as unique to you as your own fingerprint, and this is where that uniqueness really shines: segmenting and prioritizing your Master List with a relentless focus on defining and understanding your target market. Two companies with identical products, but disparity in their understanding of their target market or how they segment and prioritize leads, will execute totally unique sales strategies. Inevitably, one will outperform the other.

It is important to cast a broad net when you initially define your target market. This is not the time to disqualify any potential buyer or partner. Remember that maintaining the Master List is a Profitable Routine. A routine is not something we do once, then frame, and mount on the wall. Rather, your Master List is a living, dynamic representation of all the untapped business potential you can imagine. Update it on a regular basis. That is the first step: clearly and specifically define which organizations and which individuals would benefit from knowing more about your life-changing products and services.

But once that list has been brought up to date, you will need to further categorize and define each name based on its latent or innate sales potential. Every prospect is not created equal, and it is good stewardship to focus on those who have the greatest immediate need for your products and services. Cast a broad, highly permissive net initially. Then, rather than narrowing or limiting your field, organize it by segmenting and prioritizing your list.

This is our second type of Profitable Routine:

∞ **Segmenting** your Master List introduces critical thinking and sound judgment into selecting how, where, and when you engage every sales prospect. Each type of buyer has a unique "why"—their motivation to buy. Thus, each type of buyer requires a unique sales conversation. A former customer will not respond to your sales call the same way a new prospect responds. Segmentation recognizes that your target market is full of different types or categories of prospects. Each category requires a unique approach to address their felt needs and purchase constraints, and helps you develop irresistible offers for every buyer worthy of your time.

∞ **Prioritizing** your Master List focuses you on the quick and easy wins within each segment of your target market, allowing you to pursue and close High-Value / Low-Effort opportunities, and focus on harvesting that low-hanging fruit first. This selectiveness helps you invest your time wisely, which primes the sales pipeline by quickly filling it with bigger, better sales deals.

Segmenting

The fastest and simplest way to segment your Master List is to categorize each name as one of the four types of buyers or three types of partners.

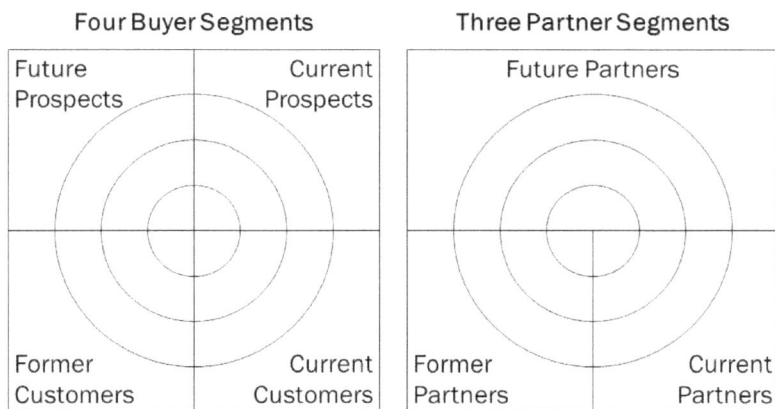

Four Buyer Segments		Three Partner Segments	
Future Prospects	Current Prospects	Future Partners	
Former Customers	Current Customers	Former Partners	Current Partners

Figure 4—Segmenting your Master List of Buyers and Partners

A future prospect (someone you have yet to engage) has different needs and expectations than a current customer. They likely need more detailed information and more time to make purchasing decisions. A future prospect may be more concerned about establishing your credibility as a vendor before they place their first order than a current or former customer.

Likewise, a former partner has a different understanding or feeling about your company and products than a current partner. Your conversation with those two individuals might be as different as night and day. Depending on your sales goals, it might be best for you to completely ignore former partners for the next ninety days and focus exclusively on building your network of partners by targeting only those names on your Master List you labeled as future partners.

Segmenting your Master List helps you predetermine how you much time you will invest to win the business of each buyer and partner. It introduces a deliberate thought process into your regular sales planning that asks: "How can I best build my book of business for the next few weeks or months? Which segments should I focus on?"

> ● ● ●
> **The power of segmentation is not in organizing the world, but in helping you to be thoughtful and deliberate in the way that you build your book of business and grow your sales revenues.**
> ● ● ●

You can certainly take this segmentation concept further, segmenting your prospects based on their particular interest in a given product, the size of their organization, and the like. However, I encourage you to focus on simplicity and immediate impact rather than data accuracy and categorization to the nth degree. The power of segmentation is not in organizing the world, but in helping you to be thoughtful and deliberate in the way that you build your book of business and grow your sales revenues.

Here is a useful statistic from the sales and marketing industry: It is seven times harder to get an order from a new prospect than it is to close repeat business with an existing customer. Not that we should focus solely on existing customers, but we need to consider that all buyers are not created equal. There is a time for relentless pursuit of new customer accounts, and there is a time to focus on current or former customers. The point of segmentation is not blind devotion to quick and easy wins, but rather to lead you through a more balanced, thoughtful, and deliberate approach to building your optimal sales plan. Rarely should a sales person focus exclusively on just one segment. On the contrary, seek a blend of opportunities from selected segments tailored to help you meet your sales goals. Segmentation is the basis of a critical element of your sales plan. It is a routine review of your Master List to consider the right strategic combination or mix of different kinds of buyers and partners to focus on for the coming weeks or months.

Large corporations invest heavily in defining marketing personas, segmenting customers based on purchasing habits, and building territories that serve specific lines of business or industries. This is fantastic—definitely a worthwhile effort when done well, and it is complete. By "complete" I mean that the needs, expectations, differences, and commonalities across the defined segments are well understood and supported throughout the entire lead-to-order lifecycle. But in my experience, few sales reps are able to leverage what the marketing department in a large corporation thinks is useful. The marketing department is typically satisfied when they can target specific demographics to generate a high volume of leads during a campaign. And the sales team is typically satisfied when they close a high volume of deals during a given quota period. Both of these groups can be satisfied, but amidst their satisfaction, plenty of untapped potential remains in the target market for competitors to continue to grow and thrive.

Rather than focusing on more complex personas or demographics –more data—the Profitable Routines approach to segmentation is a *simple, realistic, and fast* way for your team to select which buyers and partners to pursue right now.

Prioritizing

How do you prioritize names on your Master List for immediate sales results, as well as sustainable and significant long-term growth?

The Profitable Routines method of prioritizing is quick and easy, and gives you more control over your sales pipeline than simple numbering prospects in order with "1, 2, 3, …" and so on. Furthermore, the limited approach of categorizing prospects into Hot, Warm, or Cold categories is too subjective, and does not support strategic sales planning.

We need to understand two things about each potential sales opportunity: their *potential value* to our business, and the *potential effort* required to win them as a customer. Not all prospects are created equal in terms of value and effort. Some are very challenging with little reward. Others are a dream to close, almost too easy, and yet prove to be incredibly lucrative. If you've been in sales for any length of time, you will instinctively rank sales leads based on these two dimensions: value and effort.

Let's build a method on that refined, mature sales instinct. In fact, let's make it one of our Profitable Routines—a discipline or habit that we return to regularly to ensure our sales strategy remains effective and focused.

Here is the Profitable Routine for prioritizing prospects: For each name on your Master List, assign a "High-Value" or "Low-Value" designation to represent how important it would be to your business to close a deal with that person or organization. Then, in a second pass through that list, assign a "High-Effort" or "Low-Effort" designation to each name, representing the amount of work that would be required to close a deal with that person or organization.

How do you decide which are High-Value prospects and which are Low-Value? By painting a mental picture of your ideal buyer. Your ideal buyer is not an impractical fantasy, but a real-world scenario that you are likely to encounter, and that you can teach your colleagues to recognize and pursue. While we're in this vein, it is useful to make a separate list of warning signs or traits of undesirable buyers. Within a few minutes, most experienced sales people can list a dozen or two positive and negative attributes of buyers, in terms of their potential value as a customer, and the effort likely required to close a deal with them. Rank

High Value

30%	60%
High Effort	Low Effort
	10%

Low Value

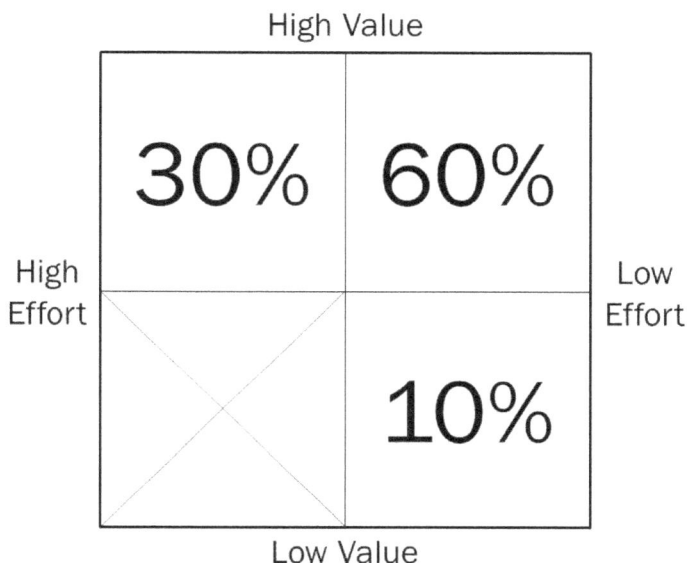

Figure 5—Prioritize your Master List based on Value and Effort

the attributes on this list in order, from most valuable to least, then consider these signals as you assign a value and effort to each name on your Master List.

To prioritize means to quickly and easily focus your efforts on the best opportunities on your Master List. The Profitable Routines method for prioritizing is fast, simple, and powerful. There is an old proverb that says, "An empty barn swept clean brings no profit." Don't get hung up on categorizing or organizing the entire world, just for the sake of orderliness. The relentless focus of Profitable Routines is to help you take quick steps to improve your sales performance.

Once you have prioritized your Master List, you need to plan how to approach the sales opportunities within each priority and segment. You must decide how much time you will spend with each priority in order to grow your book of business with the best possible strategy. As we saw with segmentation, getting clear on the untapped potential within your marketplace is just the first step.

Sixty percent of your time, energy, and attention should focus on pursuing the High-Value, Low-Effort names in your Master List. Invest thirty percent of your time in pursuing High-Value, High-Effort deals. Some people call these deals the elephants that must be "bagged", others call them the strategic accounts, or "whales", or "big fish" to be landed. These sometimes represent key strategic relationships; if that is the case, they are worthy of more detailed study to develop a uniquely tailored, ideal buying experience. In any case, the High-Value, High-Effort quadrant warrants careful management of your time and energy in order to protect your profit margin.

Low-Value, Low-Effort opportunities should get about ten percent of your time, as these often allow you to grow your book of business in breadth, gaining market share and taking territory without a lot of energy. The Low-Value, Low-Effort strategy is all about speed and efficiency, and the real harvest is the second generation, i.e., referrals. You never know where a relationship will lead. Be judicious about how much time you invest in smaller deals. This quadrant will be a bread-and-butter component of any healthy book of business. Sheer speed and momentum will help you remain profitable in this arena. Keep moving down the list of names at a steady clip. "Here's what we offer. Are you interested?" Some will be, some won't be. So what? Who's next?

As long as there is a remote possibility a prospect might buy from you in the future, there is no need to remove them from your Master List. If their response is, "Not now," simply move on. Set a Next Action—a reminder—to contact them a few months down the road, and move to the next prospect on your list.

You may choose to spend some of your spare time in working Low-Value, High-Effort deals. My recommendation is that you ignore that quadrant for the first six to twelve months, as your Profitable Routines selling system settles into place. Time spent here will dilute your sales efforts, skew your activity metrics, distract you, disappoint or discourage you, and delay or slow the onset of sales momentum. You will get a much higher return if you invest your time and energy on any of the three other quadrants of your Master List.

Each name on your Master List should be segmented and prioritized. This can be as simple as adding a few columns to your Master List where you designate each name as being a "Future Prospect," "Current Partner," "Former Customer," and so on, then also with priorities such as "High-Value," and "Low-Effort."

The next chapter explores how to design sales pursuit and retention plans, or "Ideal Buying Experiences" for each category of buyer and partner.

10

"The greatest obstacle to discovery is not ignorance,
it is the illusion of knowledge."

Daniel J. Boorstin

Routine #3: An Ideal Buying Experience

Sales trainer Jeffrey Gitomer says, "People don't like to be sold, but they love to buy."

Your Ideal Buyer doesn't care about your sales process. They don't care about your follow-up calls, milestones, probabilities, forecasts, or estimated close dates. They care about their world, their problems, and their plans - not yours. Your job is to step into their world, meet them where they are, and show them a better way. They have concerns, and most often cannot see a path around or through those concerns. They want someone to show them something "better" - something that will address those concerns. The way to do that is not by imposing your rigid sales process on your prospect, but by designing an ideal buying experience that is customer-centric and steeped in their everyday realities. This is your imperative: to deliberately engage your prospect in a shared experience centered on your product or service that builds trust and results in a significant improvement for your prospect.

The hardest work in sales is getting into your prospect's heart and mind and seeing the world as they do. It may occasionally place you at odds with your organization, your management, and your colleagues, but you will be in lock step with your prospects, ready to serve them, win them over, and close more deals.

The next essential element of an effective sales strategy is an Ideal Buying Experience. This is the internal roadmap that helps you navigate each buyer's path to trust, and helps you attract, attain, and retain the right kind of buyers and partners for your book of business. You need a simple series of steps that applies to every opportunity and prospect. - no more than eight, no fewer than four. These are the core milestones in your sales process. You may need one set for direct customers, and another to onboard a new distributor or. Just keep these steps simple and easy for everyone on your team to understand.

An Ideal Buying Experience is simply a series of steps that helps you engage, understand, educate, inspire, and make a commitment to the prospect. These steps form your core checklist or sales process for building your book of business one prospect at a time. Don't let the words "sales process" scare you. Think of this as a movie script that plays in your prospect's mind as they work with you from "Hello" to "See you again soon!" You really can (and should) keep it simple; empathy trumps complexity. Done well, this sequence of milestones will convert ad hoc, impulsive sales performance into a manageable system for success, making your business more scalable, efficient, and profitable.

One of the largest software companies in the world contacted me through a friend to ask if I would be interested in helping them redesign their technology adoption and market feedback programs. This team was responsible for engaging customers in many different roles to understand their opinions, assessments, ideas, and wish lists for features and functions in the company's commercial software products. Their target market was far more nimble, creative, and flexible than they were, and it was astonishing how quickly that market shifted

CHRISTOPHER BATES

across the Sales Maturity Model each time new software was released. This global giant was working hard to stay aligned with their target market. When I started working with them, they were already twelve to eighteen months behind several smaller companies in releasing features the marketplace was coming to expect, and they needed to show real progress to senior executives within just a few months.

We used the Profitable Routines system to first understand their target market, including their segments and priorities for buyers and partners. This company had huge databases with complex algorithms and scores of data points that they tracked about each customer. They could easily pinpoint one or two people in any role, in any company, that they wanted to engage. Their data needed some cleanup, but they seemed to have a firm grasp of their Master List, Segments, and Priorities—the first Profitable Routines.

Next, we turned to the idea of an Ideal Buying Experience. When I presented the concept on a whiteboard in a conference room at their global headquarters, the looks on their faces told me I was either way out of my league, or I had just struck a nerve. Thankfully, the latter was true, not the former. Their problem was simple: all of their processes for technology adoption and market feedback were entirely focused on getting solid feedback from their customers, in service of their own needs. They had never considered delivering value to the participants through the feedback experience. Granted, for most participants, being closely affiliated with this massive brand was flattering. Being on a first-name basis with the design team for some of the most popular software in the world is heady stuff. But in reality, it was difficult for this group to retain the same participants from year to year. Plus, the feedback from this group of participants was superficial—more critical than creative, a reaction to what was already there, instead of a strategic vision of what should be.

We worked together to create a few personas based on their Ideal Buyer for each program they managed. Then, we quickly brainstormed an Ideal Buying Experience for each persona on that list. This only took an hour or so, since this group knew their market well, but what emerged in that collaborative work session was earth-shattering for this team. When they focused on delivering value to their Ideal Buyer throughout their engagement in a market feedback program, they realized that they need to redefine their selection criteria for program participants, shifting their attention from ego-driven geeks to business-driven technology leaders. The entire team made the mental leap together. It redefined the way they engaged their target market worldwide. They suddenly shifted from myopic, complex, tactical surveys and test plans to a deeper understanding of the real-world, real-time business problems experienced by the white-hot center of their target market.

Your buyers don't need your sales process. They don't want to be sold. They want to buy.

We continued by defining a new Ideal Buying Experience for this new target market. As a result, future program participants can expect free expert help solving legitimate and unusual technology problems focused on a business objective or need. That's the value my client now offers participants. In the process, participants will meet my client's needs by helping them to envision and design new software features and functions that nobody has thought of before, putting my client back on the leading edge of the marketplace.

That single shift in perspective drove a multitude of changes, and is currently helping this massive company pull in closer to their target market than they have been in decades. The changes they are making have the potential to help them protect and grow their marketshare in a crowded, highly competitive marketplace, shaping and defining the technologies you and I will use for years to come.

CHRISTOPHER BATES

The Myopic Sales Process vs. An Ideal Buying Experience

I'd like to dramatically juxtapose these two concepts: the sales process vs. the buying experience. One is entirely seller-centric - built to support your needs. The other is entirely buyer-centric - custom built to support your prospect's needs and desires. Not surprisingly, creating an ideal buying experience is a far more effective and profitable long-term strategy than promoting a self-serving sales process.

Your buyers don't need your sales process. They don't want to be sold. They want to buy.

For most sales teams, the sales process is myopic and self-serving. It defines the steps your company has to take to drive deals forward and manage risks long enough to get contracts signed, products delivered, and money in the bank. You might have a sales process, but it doesn't reflect what your prospect needs, or how they think and feel.

Your prospect brings a very different set of expectations and frame of mind—their own. In order to win their hearts, trust, and business, you would do well to consider an Ideal Buying Experience. Begin to walk alongside them as a partner who shares their concerns, but who brings more experience and greater expertise to bear on their biggest concerns and highest priorities. The Ideal Buying Experience requires that you engage prospects with a relentless focus on meeting their needs and desires, so when the deal is closed the buyer's dominant emotion is pride of ownership.

What is your prospect's Ideal Buying Experience? Imagine all your best clients sitting in a room, and describing for you in vivid detail, from beginning to end, how they would love you to engage with them through the identification, clarification, and definition of a plan they can believe in, one that will leave their lives better than they were before. Every buyer-facing interaction and artifact (proposal, demonstration, etc.) has to serve this Ideal Buying Experience.

I am asking you to stand up, step away from your sales chair, walk around to the other side of the table, and sit down on your prospect's side of the room. Now, revisit your idea of "sales milestones" from their perspective, and create instead an Ideal Buying Experience that addresses their ideas and emotions.

As you walk a mile in your prospect's shoes, consider:

∞ How do they experience your initial contact?

∞ How do they experience your follow-up?

∞ How do they experience your sales presentation?

∞ How do they experience your order process?

∞ How do they experience your engagement with them throughout the sales process?

Get a firm grip on the most powerful perspective in business—your prospects' point of view. Then continue to help your whole company develop a better understanding of what it means to be buyer-centric with every one of your buyers and partners.

Once you have done the work of listing, categorizing, and prioritizing potential buyers, it's time to step back and look at transforming your myopic, overcomplicated, administrative sales process into a stream-lined, effective Ideal Buying Experience. This is a buyer-centric approach to sales process design. Think about each of the prospects you designated as Low-Effort, High-Value on your Master List. What is that buyer's Ideal Buying Experience for your product or service? What steps can you take, what information can you provide, what customer experience can you offer them that will make your company, your product or service and even you personally the most obvious, comfortable, appealing, attractive choice in the entire marketplace?

For instance, if your company manufactures nutritional supplements, your target market may be defined as "every human with a beating heart." That's fantastic, but within that very broad definition there are important distinctions in *how you sell* to each category of prospect. The Ideal Buying Experience for a healthy, young sports enthusiast may differ significantly from the Ideal Buying Experience for a middle-aged prospect confined to a wheelchair with debilitating diabetes. Recent research allows nutraceutical companies to market and distribute supplements that target specific disorders or diseases. So you may categorize your target market to allow you to design an Ideal Buying Experience for each segment: heart patients, fibromyalgia patients, competitive athletes, seniors, toddlers, and so on.

Many sales teams either overcomplicate or underestimate the power of a consistent sales process. If you tend to overcomplicate the sales process, it's likely because you're a natural planner. Given the chance, you could probably organize anyone or anything around you in under ten minutes. You could likely shoot from the hip and come up with a sales approach for any prospect that would be spot-on with the first draft. So, the rub for you is probably execution: picking up the phone and making the calls. We'll come back to that.

If you tend to overlook rather than overcomplicate the sales progress, well, that's a different story. "Who needs a process, anyway?" you ask. "Why be so structured and administrative? Heck, they're just people, and most of them already know me. All I need to do is have a conversation with them and we'll do business together." There are two problems with this mindset. First, you have just limited yourself to your own mental capacity - you cannot run more deals than you can keep track of in your head. Why would you leave money on the table like that, when a simple tracking system could help leverage your talent and help you double sales with a little extra effort? Second, this kind of approach means it's all about you and your personality, your timing, your availability. That means the buyer only gets your attention on your terms—not a good idea.

A Clarifying Exercise

Your next practical step in developing a sales strategy for your team is to look at each type of buyer and partner, and understand their hopes, their expectations, and the motivating factors that will propel them through the buying process. Each Ideal Buying Experience should be designed with a specific goal or outcome in mind for each prospect. To keep things simple and clear, I prefer to express each goal as a word pairs: a verb and a noun.

- ∞ **Buy Product:** these experiences usually benefit from clearly articulated benefits and simple order processes.

- ∞ **Build Trust:** these experiences usually require hefty discovery and excellent presentations that are tailored to address a specific situation. The outcome is not an order, but a partnership that results in a series of orders.

- ∞ **Engage Services:** these experiences require bona fides, stories, and symmetry between their needs and your proven capabilities.

Your goal is simple: create a list of experiences for each type of buyer and partner on your Master List. Each Ideal Buying Experience should contain four to eight stages that inform, build trust, and foster commitment. This is the core process that you will manage, so keep it simple enough to recite from memory. It might be tough to remember more than eight milestones. Fewer than four and you will likely leave some prospects behind.

Everything must be relevant to the buyer. With the technical, be technical. With the business-minded executive, be business-minded. From the metaphors you borrow to the jargon you employ, this entire process must be all about your buyer: their desires, their preferences, their needs, their world.

If you work in an established business or with a professional sales team, there may be three or four different sales processes rattling

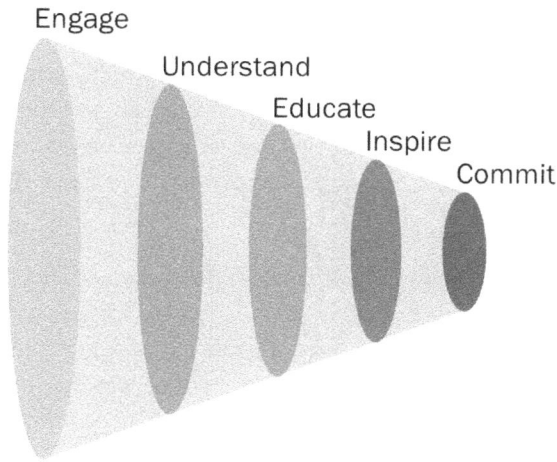

Figure 6—The Ideal Buying Experience

around your organization. Or you may be working with an old set of milestones put together by a sales manager that left the company three or four years ago and has never been challenged, questioned, or updated by the new leadership. The key question to ask is: "Is this process in sync with the felt needs, expectations, and hidden hopes of my ideal prospects?"

There are also quite a few ready-made sales methodologies available to teams and individuals. You can buy them, download them, copy and paste them. Some of these have proven results, especially those clearly created for a defined, limited market. Others simply appeal to those who want a quick fix for sales problems. Some are seen as just the latest gimmick to come along, or as a superficial attempt to stop the downhill slide of declining sales revenues.

Sales processes come in all kinds of shapes and sizes. There is no one-size-fits-all plan. How do you know you've found the right one? It expresses and supports your core beliefs about what you have to offer. It makes the cash register ring, while your new customer smiles. That is the aftereffect of an Ideal Buying Experience tailored to both your target market and your product or service.

In my work with thousands of sales leaders in hundreds of organizations, I have found some recurring themes, fundamental elements that seem to appear in every effective sales process. These ideas can serve as a simple framework to help you design an Ideal Buying Experience for your prospects.

- ∞ **Engage**—Communicate a message that resonates to the highest-priority buyers in each category of your Master List. Engage them in a dialogue with language that makes sense to them, and demonstrates that you understand their world and current needs. Offer ideas, products, and services to help them reach their goals.

- ∞ **Understand**—Ask the buyer detailed, specific questions about their current situation. Leverage your industry experience and the power of empathy to develop a list of questions that proves that you hear them—that you understand where they are, how they got there, and where they want to go. Prove to them that you care about their current situation, pressure, constraints, and needs, and that you can help.

- ∞ **Educate**—Establish your value by transforming what you learned during the Understand stage into a presentation of new and better ways to address their issues and help them move forward towards their expressed goals. Prove to them that you heard them and that your organization has the experience and capability to partner with them and move into a better future together.

- ∞ **Inspire**—Build confidence and excitement in the buyer by providing a clear path of achievable steps to help them move from where they are to where they would like to be, with your help. Connect the benefits of your offer with their expressed points of pain or need.

- ∞ **Commit**—Communicate your ability, availability, your terms and conditions, and timeframe. Say, "I will match your commitment as we move towards your goals." Make promises you can keep, and bring the buyer to the same conclusion.

The Ideal Buying Experience can be tailored to each unique type of buyer and partner. A current customer has different needs and expectations than a former customer, a future prospect, or a current prospect. Empathy is one of the most powerful characteristics of a sales leader. It is vitally important to envision the buying experience for each type of prospect you pursue. If you sell through agents, distributors, or business partners, you may want one Ideal Buying Experience to enlist new partners, and another to work with the buyers they bring to you. It might make sense to have a conversation with your High-Value, Low-Effort partners about the Profitable Routines selling system, and help them understand how to tailor a sales strategy for their book of business that will ultimately contribute to your bottom line as well.

Keep it Buyer Focused

Remember, your sales process is not about how you process internal paperwork, run transactions, or get information from prospects at various steps. Your ideal sales process is in perfect alignment with the most enjoyable purchasing process your target market could ever wish for. What does it take to attract them? To make you, your products, your services, their obvious best choice? This isn't process engineering. It is crafting an emotional and intellectual buying experience that promotes pride of ownership in your prospect from Day One, and supports their every concern.

This thoughtful, buyer-centric exercise requires a level of mature self-awareness, leadership, and honesty. Frankly, it is quite rare in most corporations.

Value the Relationship, Not Just the Transaction

People buy from you for many different reasons. What motivates one buyer may turn off another. Why do your Ideal Buyers buy from you? What are they looking for? How do you pitch, propose, or present to them? Regardless of techniques, categories, or types, it all starts in the same place: relationships. There are no shortcuts to building a relationship. You can categorize your prospects, prioritize and systemize them, but the bottom line is, they have to know and trust you.

Remember this as you design your Ideal Buying Experience. Building trust is not a matter of sending flowers, automating the sales process, or even schmoozing the client. Just as your husband or wife can tell when you're faking, so can your customers and prospects. They're smart, like you. But when you make a serious commitment to build a relationship with the person on the other side of the table, they will sense that like a bee knows nectar. Go ahead—make the commitment. It may catapult you halfway through the sales process. The rest is just paperwork.

After you have created the Ideal Buying Experience for each type of prospect, review it periodically to adjust it based on your recent interactions with your target market. Your marketplace is constantly shifting, and you will likely end up with more of a playbook than a rulebook. Practically speaking, each name on your Master List should always be tagged with the verb/noun pair that best describes their current position or stage in the Ideal Buying Experience. As you review this list periodically in daily and weekly planning sessions, you may instinctively start selecting specific prospects to pursue. This "select and pursue" discipline is our next Profitable Routine.

11

"Concentrate all your thoughts upon the work at hand.
The sun's rays do not burn until brought to a focus."

Alexander Graham Bell

Routine #4: Select and Pursue

Of the five Profitable Routines, Select and Pursue is probably the most familiar to an experienced sales representative. From your Master List, you will now select specific prospects for immediate pursuit based on what you know of your target market, the Sales Maturity Model, your segments, and your sales priorities.

This thoughtful, strategic selection of specific prospects advances your short-term, mid-term, and long-term business goals. Here, all your empathetic understanding of your target market, your subjective and objective segmentation and prioritization, and list-making converge. Now you will create (and begin to maintain) a list of sales opportunities prioritized above all others.

This is a new sub-list inside your Master List called "Active Prospects." For instance, you might have a hundred High-Value, Low-Effort prospects on your Master List—too many to pursue at once. The Select and Pursue discipline is simply a matter of tagging a few of those hundred prospects as Active, and engaging them until you either win the deal or hear them say, "not now."

When tagging prospects for immediate pursuit, consider your current sales pipeline and forecast. Build your book of business strategically by including a mix of prospects with various value/effort designations, segments, industries, length of their sales cycle, and potential size of their order.

A wise sales strategy helps you select and pursue those Ideal Buyers who can sustain your business as it shifts along the Sales Maturity Model.

I once worked with a large health care company to help them implement a new customer relationship management system. This corporation was spending millions of marketing dollars each year to generate new lists of leads for their sales organization to pursue. Their sales reps were almost drowning in business potential, simply because they had no practical system that would allow them to tag or rank the thousands of names on their marketing lists. Instead, they had to call each lead in turn with no proactive prioritization. Sales became a pure numbers game that resulted in high burnout and staff turnover.

It was a fairly big project for this organization to change the way they pursue marketing leads. A lot of people would need to sign off on the new business processes and systems to support the change; more than a thousand sales reps were involved, hundreds of managers, and scores of administrative staff. Yet in the end, their solution was simple and elegant. While it honored the marketing department's rich collections of demographic data on each lead, the core of the new system was a feature that allowed each sales rep to select prospects they wanted to pursue from their lists, based on any number of attributes, and tag them as their "Active" sales pursuits. Then, they could review a shortened list of those active prospects, make calls, keep notes, and track their progress through the sales cycle. The entire sales team embraced the new software quickly, simply because they relished this strategic new capability.

But you don't need an expensive or complicated software system to get the same result. You can set up and manage the entire Profitable

Routines system on a few blank sheets of paper or a simple spreadsheet. It was the new concept and capability, not the software, that freed my client's sales representatives to focus on reaching their untapped business potential.

Prospecting across the Sales Maturity Model

Selling in a Windfall market is largely a reactive exercise. The sales volume is high, buyers are beating a path to your door, and the objective is to take orders as quickly as possible and move on to the next call. But at some point your steady stream of orders is likely to taper off, sometimes rather suddenly. During Windfall, it would be a wise sales strategy to select and pursue Ideal Buyers who can sustain your business as it shifts along the Sales Maturity Model from Windfall to Hunter. This requires thoughtful planning, and a good understanding of the characteristics that make those buyers ideal to help you navigate this transition. Who, among your buyers, can sustain a volume of repeat orders from month-to-month or quarter-to-quarter? Who might be interested in an extended service and support relationship that will keep you engaged until your next product version is released and you can sell them an upgraded edition? Who has become dependent on your products and services as a key part of their livelihood? Who relies on you now as part of their supply chain? Who has placed initial orders in smaller quantities, yet has a larger demand or user base that could benefit from even more of your products or services? Tailor these criteria to your business, then refer to them as you select those customers who can help you navigate the transition from Windfall to Hunter.

For Hunters, routinely selecting and pursuing prospects is second nature. You hunt or you starve. When game is plentiful, selection and pursuit are fairly easy to accomplish. But the Hunter's Achilles heel is acute hunger. Once the cupboards are empty and game is no longer plentiful, you choke back panic, and any signs of life on the trail can cause a frenetic crashing pursuit that ends up scaring off the very prospect you desperately need to engage. A more deliberate, methodical approach can bring better results. As you review your Master List, ask yourself which areas of your book of business need immediate or near-term growth. Do you need to expand by adding new customers, or capitalize on existing relationships by focusing on garnering repeat business from current customers?

Farmers make sales look easy, but in fact they are simply reaping the rewards of long hours of wise investments in their target market. The key to selection and pursuit for a Farmer is to work both smart and hard. Once you have an established book of business, there may be a temptation to sit back and become reactive. But the only profitable condition for reactive selling is Windfall. Stasis, not hunger, is the insidious enemy of a Farmer. A Farmer's work is seasonal, but no less intense than a Hunter's. For a Farmer, the Master List is viewed through the lens of profitable long-term relationships. A Farmer is more interested in opening up new channels for sales revenue than in pursuing a single deal. Thus, you may want to make more balanced or similar investments in each segment and priority for buyers and partners. The reputation of the Farmer is important to the marketplace. Therefore, you may decide that pursuing former buyers and partners is as important to your sales strategy as current or new buyers and partners.

The Pursuit

Ideally, less than twenty percent of your time each week is spent on administrative planning tasks, even strategic ones like updating your Master List, selecting prospects for pursuits, segmenting and prioritizing, and the like. Eighty percent of your time is best dedicated to actually executing those strategic plans. Spend face-to-face time with prospects and customers. Build presentations and have conversations that are steeped in their points of pain, their dreams, and their hope that they might someday find a better way.

The tasks related to building a Profitable Routines sales plan are designed to bring focus to your efforts. Add to that plan your passion for your products, your confidence in your company's ability to deliver, and your daily hard work as you pursue meaningful conversations with prospects. When all of these elements combine, success is simply a matter of time.

Only one step remains. To really hit your stride in sales, all of this pursuit planning must result in a new task with a due date for every active prospect you have selected as worthy of your time. Now you are prepared to examine the fifth Profitable Routine: Next Actions.

12

"Have you ever thought…about whatever man builds,
that all of man's industrial efforts, all his computations and calculations,
all the nights spent over working draughts and blueprints, invariably
culminate in the production of a thing whose sole and guiding
principle is the ultimate principle of simplicity?"

Antoine de Saint Exupery
Wind, Sand and Stars

Routine #5: Next Actions

Next Actions is the fifth essential discipline in the Profitable Routines selling system. Every prospect, partner, and sales opportunity should have a "next task" assigned, with a due date and desired outcome. Having a next action planned for every buyer and partner is the critical link between sales strategy and sales tactics. This is the daily sales discipline that drives business steadily forward toward monthly and quarterly goals.

Without a Next Action defined for every high priority prospect, partner, or sales deal, you're leaving behind low-hanging fruit—potentially thousands of dollars in sales, not to mention referrals that could lead you to new buyers and business partners, and the goodwill that leads to respect and acceptance from the marketplace you serve.

A Next Action is a single task, not a process. It is a single conversation or interaction, not a series of steps. It is the smallest unit of work in your daily or weekly sales planning and activity management. Be sure to make each Next Action specific and achievable; "Call Steve on Friday to discuss his weekly volume and unique needs for waste management services."

A community credit union contacted me recently with the desire to improve follow-up for members who expressed interest in mortgage rates while working with a teller in a branch. At the time, they had no system in place to ensure that these prospects would have a follow-up call, or that the teller would get credit or compensation for the upsell referral. A new or refinanced mortgage was one of the most profitable products this firm had to offer, so if we could solve this problem and improve close rates, the additional revenue could help fund other strategic growth campaigns for the next few quarters.

Every prospect, partner, and sales opportunity should have a Next Action assigned, with a due date and desired outcome.

We quickly worked through the Profitable Routines sales plan, defining their target market, with segments and priorities. For this group, the lights came on when we discussed two areas: the Ideal Buying Experience and Next Actions. Without a tracking system to ensure solid follow-up on mortgage referrals, credit union members might wait several weeks to hear from the credit union. After hearing nothing, many moved on to apply for their mortgage elsewhere. We walked through the mortgage referral process from "Hello" to "Goodbye," from the prospect's point of view.

Like most teams, these professionals were experts in the internal application process; they could run a flawless business transaction. However, as we discussed the Ideal Buying Experience, many of them commented that they had never considered the experience of a new prospective mortgage applicant or examined entire process through their eyes. We made a list of bottlenecks and breakdowns in the follow-up and application process. The team collaborated across departments to design a new, member-centric Ideal Buying Experience specifically for the mortgage scenario.

Next, we worked with their I.T. team to develop a simple tracking system to capture and automatically route new mortgage leads to the right internal team, showing each teller the number of referrals they'd generated that month. In the weeks that followed, they trained their tellers and the new tracking system was rolled out to branches throughout the community.

Results were immediate. With the new focus on mortgage referrals, their sales pipeline swelled, which put strain on the mortgage team's ability to handle the new business volume. But by this time, business leaders were using the Profitable Routines sales plan as a new set of tools to review and evaluate other sales and marketing experiences, and they were able to successfully address the bottlenecks and breakdowns on their own.

Name	Type	Segment	Value	Effort	Status	Stage	Next Action	Due
Mike Karaoke	Partner	Future Partner	High	Low	Active	Educate	Demo products	January 8
Sue Mi	Customer	Current Customer	High	Low	Active	Understand	Find decision criteria	January 5
Delta Retail	Partner	Former Partner	High	Low	Active	Inspire	Review client list	January 7
Charlie Ind	Partner	Current Partner	High	Medium	Active	Commit	Set next quarter goals	March 15
Willie Makit	Customer	Future Prospect	High	Medium	Active	Engage	Company/product intro	January 20
Sarah Bellum	Customer	Current Customer	High	High				
Pete Moss	Partner	Future Partner	High	Medium				
Acme Corp	Customer	Current Prospect	Medium	Low				
Bravo, Inc.	Customer	Former Customer	Medium	Low				
Natalie Dressed	Customer	Future Prospect	Medium	Low				
Echo Expo	Customer	Current Customer	Medium	Low				
Casey Deeya	Partner	Current Partner	Low	Low				
Tracey Drawer	Customer	Current Customer	Low	Medium				
Mark Onwall	Customer	Current Prospect	Low	High				

Figure 7—Your Master List, Segmented and Prioritized, with a Stage and Next Action for every Active Opportunity

The Next Actions concept is arguably the easiest of our five Profitable Routines core disciplines. Yet surprisingly, I have found that only the top salespeople in any given company have truly internalized this habit and made it automatic. If your mind cannot rest easy in the midst of pursuing several large sales deals, if you have trouble keeping all the balls in the air, or if you're not sure what to do next, for whom, and when, then your sales capacity is severely limited. Things begin to fall through the cracks, important things that your prospects care about. The Next Actions discipline will allow you to settle into a lower-stress cadence week after week, expanding your capacity to sell, but letting you rest easy in the knowledge that you've forgotten nothing, that you know what to do next with each sales pursuit, and that these details are safely captured and tracked in a reliable, accessible system.

The Next Actions you plan for each buyer and partner, along with task descriptions and due dates, are the final additions to your Master List, and are the most dynamic and frequently updated elements on that list. Most sales professionals use productivity management tools like customer relationship management (CRM) software to track and manage this kind of information. CRM systems typically include many more features and track far more information about buyers than we cover in the Profitable Routines system. And they often impose stricter controls and greater complexity on the way sales deals are managed. Done well, CRM can accelerate your sales productivity. Done poorly, it replaces vital face-time with prospects with administrative screen time, as you are forced to spend hours every week making the data look "just right."

Remember, your goal with Profitable Routines is not to organize the whole world, but to serve your target market by selling the best products available, to the best prospects, in the best possible way. The simpler your tracking systems, the sooner you will achieve a net gain in sales productivity.

13

"My doctrine is that 'Sales fixes everything.'
As long as you're making sales, you're still in the game.
Without sales, all the strategic stuff like partnerships,
technology and vision mean nothing."

Guy Kawasaki

The Punch Line

Congratulations! You now have all five elements of an effective sales planning system. Let's review.

The Master List

The Master List contains the names of your current, former, and future buyers and partners. You can and should add new names to your Master List at any time, but you can also set aside time to deliberately review and refine this list, prioritizing each name by business value and effort to pursue. This list should also include the primary contact information for those buyers and partners you have selected to pursue immediately. This list is the core, the foundation, of your Profitable Routines sales plan, and should be updated each week.

Segment and Prioritize

All prospects are not created equal. There are four types of buyers and three types of partners, each with a unique set of expectations and needs. When you anticipate and address their hopes and needs, you become faster and more effective at meeting their expectations and closing the deal. By focusing sixty percent of your time on High-Value, Low-Effort business opportunities, you begin to fill your pipeline with immediate revenue relief. This buys you the time to pursue High-Value, High-Effort deals that are strategic in nature, or Low-Value, Low-Effort deals that might lead to referrals or other recognition. Each name on your list should carry three designations to help you manage your sales efforts: Segment (Future Prospects, Current Prospects, Current Customers, Former Customers, Current Partners, Future Partners, or Former Partners), Value (High or Low), and Effort (High or Low). These designations should be reviewed once a month, and more frequently for new names on your Master List or those you are pursuing right now.

An Ideal Buying Experience

An Ideal Buying Experience is a buyer-centric sales process defined as four to eight stages or shared experiences that you create for each prospect. Each experience springs from a deep understanding of the buyer's worldview, and is designed to excite, motivate, and substantially address the needs and expectations of the buyer throughout the sales process. Your Ideal Buying Experience will be documented separately from your Master List, but each name on that list is in the midst of one of the stages you have defined. That stage should be noted for each buyer and partner on your Master List.

Select and Pursue

Review the names on your Master List and select prospects to designate as "Active" pursuits. Deselect prospects who you no longer believe to be worth the investment of your time; you will be reactive to these prospects, serving them well, but matching their level of commitment to a business partnership with you. Be strategic about achieving a balance of prospects across all segments, and within each priority. If you are building a book of business in a Hunter market, you should focus immediately on Current Prospects and Future Prospects, investing at least sixty percent of your time and energy on High-Value, Low-Effort names within those segments. However, if you are established as a Farmer and concerned primarily with protecting your existing book of business from competitors, you might choose to focus on Current Customers primarily, and pursue a blend of both High-Value, Low-Effort and High-Value, High-Effort accounts.

Next Actions

A Next Action is a concrete task or activity with a desired outcome and due date. You need one of these for every prospect and opportunity on your Master List. These are the actions drive the Ideal Buying Experience forward, day-by-day, through a series of interactions with each buyer or partner. Remember, every person on your list and every deal in your pipeline must have a Next Action assigned. This is the final column beside each name on your Master List.

Sales is hard work, and it's nearly impossible to succeed without a sales plan that focuses and maximizes all of your effort. The whole idea of Profitable Routines is to provide a system to help you consistently build profitable relationships and grow revenue. It is simple, fast and methodical, and helps you to plan all the practical steps that will lead you to achieve your sales goals. When you use the Profitable Routines system consistently, you will enjoy a perpetual backlog of untapped business potential that is quantified and readily available to you as a collection of "pursuits-in-waiting."

Imagine how effective this system could be if you tailored it to your unique market, products and services, and sales team over the next four weeks, then tested and leveraged those variations to your advantage. Wouldn't that be something? An incalculably deep well of potential is yours as you begin to put your Profitable Routines selling system into place.

Plan your work, and work your plan. The next section will demonstrate how to put these tools to work as a competitive advantage.

Part Three

ADOPT, ADAPT, AND ACCELERATE

14

"To achieve great things, two things are needed:
a plan, and not quite enough time."

Leonard Bernstein

A Four-Week Plan

Profitable Routines is a flexible framework to help you create and manage an optimal sales plan based on your current sales environment. Working through the following exercises will produce a robust, personalized sales plan to carry you through the next few months, paving the way for you to meet or exceed your sales quota.

In the first two sections of the book, you studied the essential elements of a successful sales strategy. In this third

My goal is to make every hour you give to this plan worth twenty hours of time you might spend selling without a clear plan, method, or strategy

and final section, you will walk step-by-step through a plan to help you tailor the Profitable Routines system to your products, company, and target market.

I assume you are a busy professional with deadlines, demands on your time, and a constant battle with the tyranny of the urgent. I can understand any resistance you might have to taking the time to develop a sales strategy while you are driving hard to meet your quota for the month, quarter, or year's end. You hesitate to take your foot off the gas pedal, so to speak, to look at the road map. In designing this plan, I have taken into account the reality of your long hours and full schedule in the sales trenches.

There is no reason you cannot experience the same success as my other clients. Given the book in your hands, you have only to apply and use these ideas in order to achieve similar results. Many of us hate to admit that we need accountability and discipline, but we really do our best work when those elements are present. You have the plan; now I'm asking you to create your own accountability, and apply your own disciplined effort.

This four-week plan is designed to help you see immediate benefits and payoff, supporting your current efforts to reach your immediate sales objectives. My goal is to make every hour you give to this plan worth twenty hours of the time you might spend selling without a clear strategy.

I love salespeople. I love working with salespeople. I love talking with salespeople. I love your stories, your drive, your street smarts, and your determined optimism. In over a decade of work with thousands of sales professionals at more than a hundred companies, I have seen the Profitable Routines system help sales teams grow their revenues within a few short months. But information and inspiration can only take you so far toward your goals. To make real progress, you need a simple, straightforward method to help you stay on track with your sales efforts week after week, month after month, until you internalize these new habits. This will be you focus over the next four weeks as you adopt, adapt, and accelerate.

A Flexible Framework

Energy management is crucial to sales execution. You can't always be up. You can't always be certain, nor always optimistic. You can't always have the right attitude for closing, for dealing with every possible client situation. Salespeople know how to sell, but few do it consistently. Nobody can be a hundred percent all the time. You need a selling system that allows you to maximize your energy level at any time, plowing through lows and capitalizing on highs as you sell your way through the week.

Human nature renders rigid sales methodologies inadequate; nobody likes an automaton. The methodology should serve you, not the other way around. You need a system that is flexible, simple, and familiar. One that uses whatever time and energy you can afford to maximize your selling efforts for consistent results.

Is that possible? Absolutely.

You can create a flexible framework for success in sales that has enough structure to make sure nothing falls through the cracks, and enough flexibility to make it easy to use over the long haul. These Profitable Routines are the basics of executing sales, of getting new leads, of prospecting, of opportunity management, of presentations, closing, managing transactions, forecasting, and preparation. These core essential disciplines are the same for every salesperson in the world, regardless of what product, company, team, or market you serve.

"Well, we have tried everything," some folks argue. "Our situation is so unique that no methodology will work for us." This is often the argument of someone unwilling to change, or more specifically, someone unwilling to reconsider their self-limiting assumptions. There certainly are unique attributes that define your company, your products, your team, your buyers, and the market you serve. Those unique attributes differentiate you from competitors, for better or worse. But if you look beneath those variables, you realize that every successful salesperson uses the same basic selling system. You must master this core framework (adopt), tailor it to your needs (adapt), and then put it to work (accelerate).

For Example...

It is Monday morning, first of the month. You just wrapped up last month with a final push to get across the goal line and make your numbers. You are exhausted after reaching quota, but you need to know how best to set yourself up for success this month.

Or perhaps it is the middle of the month, Thursday afternoon, after lunch. You're exhausted after cold calling all morning. You need something to do that you know will help you move your overall sales strategy forward, but you know you're not at the top of your game right now to talk to buyers.

On Tuesday afternoon, you make a big sale. Yes! You have this huge deal in your pocket and three weeks left to go in the quarter. Your confidence is high. You're energetic. You want to celebrate, but first you want to see if you can slam down a few more sales. Enthusiasm is contagious. Success breeds success. You know that now is the right time to make a few more calls to the hot prospects in your sales pipeline - you are so wired, there is no way they could say "no."

With some simple, essential disciplines, the core framework of a sales methodology in place, you will always have something to do—a Next Action on your list or a Profitable Routine—that matches your maximum possible performance, any hour of any day.

The truth is that most salespeople are not naturally methodical. They are inspirational. They are enthusiastic. They are distractible, and they are far more relational than transactional. But if you have a core framework of the essential disciplines for a rock solid sales strategy, you can put it to work for you and develop Profitable Routines that will work within your strengths and weaknesses to support your efforts and bring success.

Watch that first step!

I challenge you to make a renewed commitment to your team today, a commitment that is fully aligned with your own professional and financial goals in sales. Here is the commitment: to invest ninety minutes each week over the next four weeks in building and adopting your own Profitable Routines sales plan.

There is no way this system will fail you. It's time to test it, let it stand on its own legs. Put yourself in a position where you cannot lose. It is far better to end this four-week period having given your best effort, than to fall back into the fits and starts of those reactive, half-planned sales habits that have consistently produced inconsistent results.

If you are ready to make this commitment, pick up the phone and let a friend or business colleague know what you are up to. "Signing up" publicly is an important psychological trick you can play on yourself to cement your engagement in this process.

Here is your first assignment: set an appointment for your first ninety-minute work session with the Profitable Routines system. You will need a time and a place to do this work, some place quiet and free from distractions. You will need this book, a pen, and a blank notebook to start working through the steps and create your own winning sales strategy.

Do it now. Block out an appointment on your calendar to work solo for ninety minutes on your own personal sales strategy, using what you've learned here.

15

Week One: Start your Master List

Your goal for Week One is to create the first draft of your Master List, then to quickly segment and prioritize those names to find immediate sales opportunities to pursue this week. Once you have finished the exercises in this section, you will have the foundation for your Profitable Routines sales plan. You will then be able to build on this during weeks two, three, and four, to adopt all five Profitable Routines core disciplines. These exercises will each require about an hour of your time, and will help you "release the brakes," defining and pursuing the untapped sales potential that is available to you right now.

Exercise One: Create Your Master List (30 minutes)

Our first Profitable Routine is the care and feeding of your Master List. Remember, the purpose of the Master List is to *identify everyone you could possibly want to engage in a conversation* about your products and services. In this section, you'll create just the first draft.

Take out a blank piece of paper, and write the word "Buyers" at the top. Draw two lines—one down the center of the page, the other across the middle—to divide the paper into four quadrants. Label the top left segment, "Future Prospects." Label the top right, "Current Prospects." Label the lower left segment, "Former Customers," and the lower right segment, "Current Customers." Next, brainstorm the names of some of your prospects within each of these four segments. Write those names down in each quadrant as quickly as possible.

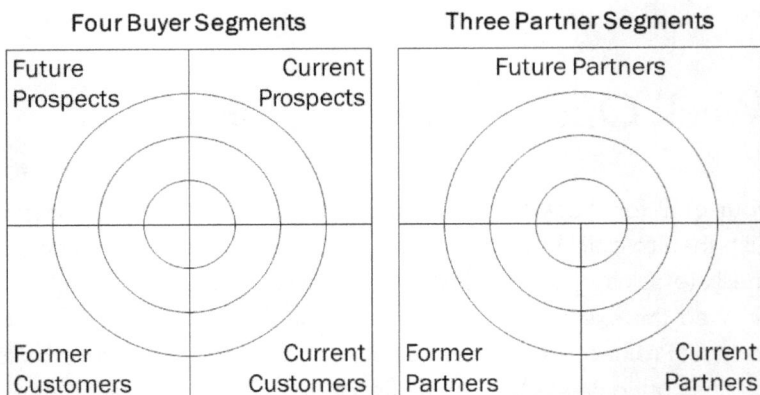

Four Buyer Segments   **Three Partner Segments**

Future Prospects	Current Prospects	Future Partners	
Former Customers	Current Customers	Former Partners	Current Partners

Remember that a healthy Master List will include all kinds of buyers: brand new prospects, current customers, former customers, and future prospects—those you would like to contact. Be sure you have a solid list of names in each of these segments. Also, keep in mind that maintaining this Master List is one of your Profitable Routines, so you will cover this ground again. Any names you miss in this first pass will eventually make it onto the list.

A month or two from now, you may want to plan a referral campaign or lead generation effort to fill your Master List with new leads. But a campaign like that is a more involved process that should be triggered by a chronic lack of names in the "Future Prospects" segment of your

Master List. For now, we want to keep things simple.

Here are a few sources for names that you might add to your Master List:

∞ Personal and professional contact lists, such as email and social media networks

∞ Current customers, especially those you have not contacted within the last six months

∞ Sales prospects you failed to close

∞ Deals your competition dropped during their sales process or in service and support

∞ Business cards or leads from a trade show

For now, focus on brainstorming for the next few minutes, writing down as many names or categories as possible from memory in each segment. Move fast. Keep your pen moving until each segment on the paper is nearly full or you've exhausted your mental lists. Don't get bogged down with questions or decisions about where you will store this information or what kind of software or tracking system you might use. We will talk about tracking systems later.

Next, turn the sheet of paper over, and label the top of this page, "Partners."

Divide this page into three segments by drawing a line horizontally first, dividing the paper in half, then drawing a second line from the center of the page to the bottom of the page. Label the top section of the page "Future Partners." Label the lower left segment "Former Partners." And label the lower right segment "Current Partners."

Now quickly list as many business partners as you can in each segment names of people and organizations that you would love to work with in the coming six to eighteen months. When your pen stops moving for ten seconds, take a break and move to the next segment. This will keep your mind moving and shifting. Another trick:

think about your most successful experiences with partners over the past several years. Where can you find more partners like that? Feel free to write down categories or lead sources, not just the actual proper names of partners. Anything is permissible as you define and document the untapped potential in your target market. When all three segments are pretty full, put down your pen.

Congratulations! You just created the first draft of your Master List, the core of your sales focus. This is your backlog, the list of untapped potential that you will reach into later to open the floodgates for revenue-generating conversations. But your Master List will continue to adapt, grow, and change as your focus, perspective, and understanding of your target market expands and shifts. You'll come back to it next week!

Exercise Two: Segment and Prioritize (20 minutes)

The second Profitable Routine is Segmenting and Prioritizing. Once it is mature and up to date, your Master List should contain more leads than you could follow up in a year. If it doesn't yet, no worries. Over the next month, you will revisit that list every week and continue to brainstorm new prospects and lead sources.

The names in your Master List are already segmented according to their positions on the diagrams you drew on the paper. So, how do you efficiently and effectively prioritize these sales deals or prospects? Let's move as quickly as possible through this exercise, using the information you have right now to categorize each name on your Master List, both buyers and partners.

Glance over your Master List again. Remember the two-by-two grid for prioritizing based on value and effort? The x axis represents "Effort"— the amount of time and energy you must invest to win this business. The y axis represents "Value"—the short- and long-term benefits of closing this deal, or having this client in your book of business.

Now prioritize each name on your Master List, first by Value, then by Effort. You might feel you need to prequalify your prospects in order to gain a little more information before you prioritize them. But the most effective sales leaders prioritize, then reprioritize, then reprioritize again. It is a constant discipline for them, as it will be for you. We will cover this ground again in good time - nothing here is set in stone. You can freely run through this list today, prioritizing each prospect based on what you know right now, knowing that you will soon have the opportunity to reevaluate each priority. Remember, done is better than perfect!

Exercise Three: Select and Pursue (10 minutes)

It is time to put this new information to work. Use your brand-new Master List with defined segments and priorities to guide your prospecting and sales calls for the coming week.

Pull out your Master List. Using whatever designation you prefer (stars, asterisks, underlining, highlighters), specifically mark prospective buyers and partners you intend to pursue in the next week.

Don't waste time or tears on Low-Value, High-Effort opportunities and prospects until you are a well-established Farmer in your marketplace. There is far too much untapped potential among the prospects that rank higher in value, and lower in effort. Here are the guidelines:

∞ Sixty percent of your time should be invested in High-Value, Low-Effort opportunities and prospects.

∞ Twenty to thirty percent of your time should be invested in High-Value, High-Effort opportunities and prospects.

∞ Ten to twenty percent of your time should be invested in Low-Value, Low-Effort opportunities and prospects.

These percentages are just suggestions. Profitable Routines does not require rigid adherence to a formula. Take full ownership of your sales plan, and adjust the amount of effort you believe each prospect needs and deserves given your present circumstances and future vision. This is where your sales plan begins to reflect your unique sales environment—the Sales Maturity Model—and your specific goals.

Mark these prospects clearly to indicate that they are now on your Active Prospects list. Now, pick up the phone, and start making calls to those Active Prospects. It's time to sell!

Optional Exercise: Paper to Spreadsheet (30 minutes)

If you are a systems person, it may annoy you to think about managing your sales plan on paper rather than in an electronic data system. So in this optional exercise, you will see how powerful the Profitable Routines selling system when you bring all five core elements together in a single spreadsheet.

First, take out your Master List worksheet. Now, create a new blank spreadsheet on your computer, and label eight columns across the top: Name, Type, Segment, Value, Effort, Status, Stage, Next Action, and Due, like this:

Name	Type	Segment	Value	Effort	Status	Stage	Next Action	Due
Mike Karaoke	Partner	Future Partner	High	Low	Active	Educate	Demo products	January 8
Sue Mi	Customer	Current Customer	High	Low	Active	Understand	Find decision criteria	January 5
Delta Retail	Partner	Former Partner	High	Low	Active	Inspire	Review client list	January 7
Charlie Ind.	Partner	Current Partner	High	Medium	Active	Commit	Set next quarter goals	March 15
Willie Makit	Customer	Future Prospect	High	Medium	Active	Engage	Company/product intro	January 20
Sarah Bellum	Customer	Current Customer	High	High				
Pete Moss	Partner	Future Partner	High	Medium				
Acme Corp	Customer	Current Prospect	Medium	Low				
Bravo, Inc.	Customer	Former Customer	Medium	Low				
Natalie Dressed	Customer	Future Prospect	Medium	Low				
Echo Expo	Customer	Current Customer	Medium	Low				
Casey Deeya	Partner	Current Partner	Low	Low				
Tracey Drawer	Customer	Current Customer	Low	Medium				
Mark Onwall	Customer	Current Prospect	Low	High				

Next, on the left side of your spreadsheet, in the Name column, type in the names of those buyers and partners from your Master List paper worksheet. In the Segment column, note whether each prospect is a Current Prospect, Future Prospect, Current Customer, Former Customer, Future Partner, Former Partner, or Current Partner.

In the Stage column, note the prospect's current stage in their Ideal Buying Experience. For this, you can refer to the milestones you defined in our earlier exercise, or use the five stages in the core Ideal Buying Experience: Engage, Understand, Educate, Inspire, and Commit.

In the Next Action column, write down a specific task you need to complete in order to move that prospect forward to the next stage in the Buying Experience. Finally, put a due date beside that task.

Take a moment now to review your work. Imagine how your business might benefit if you simply completed each Next Action you have listed in the spreadsheet.

You may also want to add columns for email address, phone number, and notes. But setting up sales tracking systems in spreadsheets or software can be a slippery slope for a front-line sales rep. If you find this line of work fascinating (or a way to avoid prospecting), you may want to inquire about openings in your I.T. department. Your job is to sell, not to systemize. Consider how much administrative work is required to get you focused on the best opportunities in your sales pipeline, and do just that much work. Then get back to selling. Keep it simple.

16

Week Two: The Buyer's Perspective

This week, invest an hour or two in deliberately examining your ideal buyers and partners, their characteristics, hopes, expectations, and unique perspectives. This will pay off big time in every thoughtful sales conversation you have over the next few weeks. After completing these exercises, you will be able to quickly distinguish an ideal buyer or partner from a less-than-ideal prospect, and articulate the characteristics of an ideal prospect versus a high-maintenance or Low-Value prospect.

Exercise One: Five Attributes of an Ideal/ Tough Buyer (15 minutes)

You will need your Master List for this exercise. Look over the list of buyers you prioritized as High-Value, Low-Effort. Consider for a moment the specific attributes you used to prioritize those names. You used some combination of subjective and objective criteria to determine whether each name was high- or Low-Value, and high- or Low-Effort. What were those criteria?

Now, take out a blank sheet of paper, and divide the page into two columns. Above the left column write, "Ideal Buyers." Label the right column, "Tough Buyers." Quickly brainstorm the attributes you used—or feel you should use—to evaluate each potential buyer on your Master List. Write down the telltale signs of an easy sale in the left-hand column. What kind of buyers do you absolutely love to work with?

Next, list the challenging traits of tough buyers in the right-hand column. What slows down a deal? What complicates conversations, or makes it difficult to build trust or get paperwork completed? Remember to stay focused on the traits and attributes of your buyers and prospects, not your own organization's limitations or needs.

Once you have at least ten attributes in each column, stop and number them in order of significance, with the number one attribute of an ideal buyer being the most important. Use the same numbering system for tough buyers: number one is the primary indicator of a tough buyer, number two is less significant, and so on.

Next, take out a clean sheet of paper, and rewrite your notes in a legible, easy-to-read format. Save this chart so you can refer to, adjust, and revise these attributes over the coming weeks.

Exercise Two: Five Attributes of an Ideal/Tough Partner (15 minutes)

Next, take a few moments to look over your Master List of partners, paying special attention to those you designated as High-Value, Low-Effort. Ask yourself the same questions about partners that you did in the last exercise regarding buyers. Consider the subjective and objective criteria you used to determine whether each partner was high- or Low-Value, and high- or Low-Effort. What were those criteria? Use the back side of your Ideal/Tough Buyers worksheet to create an identical chart to list the attributes of your Ideal Partners and Tough Partners.

Quickly make a list of the attributes you used to prioritize each of the partners in your Master List. Note which of those attributes serve as clues to help you identify a great partner. Are they proactive—do they call you more often than you call them? Do they have a large existing clientele, or a high volume of transactions that compliments your target market?

Now consider those partners that are tough or unproductive to work with. What are the specific characteristics that make those partners less desirable?

After you have listed ten or twenty attributes in each column, go back and rank them numerically, from one (most significant attribute) to ten or twenty. Now transfer your notes to the back of your more legible Buyer Attributes chart, with the "Partner Attributes" label at the top.

Exercise Three: Design an Ideal Buying Experience for Current Prospects (30 minutes)

Quick refresher: An ideal buying experience is a series of steps that helps you engage, understand, educate, inspire, and make a commitment to the prospect. To get started, let's look at each category of buyer in your Master List. Take a few minutes now to review the four segments we defined earlier: Current Customer, Former Customer, Current Prospect, and Future Prospect. Now, on a blank sheet of paper, list these five buying experience milestones in sequence:

- ∞ Engage
- ∞ Understand
- ∞ Educate
- ∞ Inspire
- ∞ Commit

At the top of the page write, "Ideal Buying Experience for Current Prospects."

Now, review the names of the Current Prospects on your Master List. Take a few minutes to consider prospects' real and felt needs at each of the five steps. For now, forget everything you know about the administrative tasks of running a transaction, and simply focus on the buying experience from your prospect's point of view. As you do this, make notes beside each milestone regarding the specific steps, conversations, interactions, and turning points that you and the buyer must work through in order to move from initial introduction to closed sale. What are the bare basics you need to run the transaction? What does the buyer need to hear, see, feel, or experience in order to keep moving forward? Break those experiences or interactions down into milestones or stages, with your needs and theirs side by side.

Remember: This is just the first draft of an Ideal Buying Experience for Current Prospects. The most important thing about this exercise is not that your new buyer-centric buying process is perfect and complete, but that every note you make is steeped in deep empathy and understanding of each prospect's needs and expectations.

It might be useful to create a timeline for Current Prospects—a sample sales cycle to help you envision the entire process from beginning to end. If you do this, consider the two different perspectives of this process: the seller's experience, and the buyer's experience.

Many sales representatives find it important to designate the first milestone as "New" or "Unqualified Lead." This allows them to track every lead in a single system by having a designation that basically equates to, "I haven't started working on this one yet." If you choose this path, it would make sense to call your second milestone something like "Qualified" or "Engaged," indicating you have started working on the deal and it is in progress. Often, the final stage is labeled "Win!" or something similar. This allows you to track those deals that have closed successfully. Obviously, won deals would no longer appear with an "Active" designation, but it is encouraging, and often administratively beneficial for reconciling compensation payments, to track those sales you have closed successfully.

Exercise Four: Review and Refresh your Master List (30 minutes)

It is time to put this new information to work for you immediately. The next exercise will give you greater clarity and confirmation of the focus for your sales work in the coming week.

First, revisit the priorities you assigned last week to the buyers and partners in your Master List. Why revisit those designations? Because you have better insight and clearer understanding of your target market now. Having completed the last three exercises, you have a more specific concept of what makes ideal buyers and partners higher-value and lower-effort than the other names on your list. To ensure you are pursuing the right buyers and partners, you need to review the priorities you assigned subjectively last week, and update them based on your newly defined objective attributes you defined in Exercise Three.

Refer to the final lists you made in Exercises One and Two, where you defined the attributes of ideal buyers and partners versus tough buyers and partners. Take a pass through your Master List now and, if needed, update the value and effort designations beside each name.

Quickly review each name in your Master List and update your designations of Active Prospects. It's okay to drop a few prospects that you had designated as Active last week, even if you didn't have time to pursue them. Profitable Routines is not about finishing everything on your list, it's about focusing on the best things on your list. Besides, given your clearer understanding of ideal versus tough prospects, you probably want to refresh that list of Active prospects this week anyway, to ensure you are focusing on the best potential in your Master List. Refresh that list again next week, and the following week, and every week.

Finally, assign a sales milestone to each Active prospect in your Master List, based on the Ideal Buying Experience you created for Current Prospects in Exercise Three. In the coming weeks, you will design additional Ideal Buying Experiences for each segment in your Master List. But for now, just focus on Active names in the "Current Prospects" segment. Review those names now, and beside each, write the name of the milestone that represents the current sales stage for that prospect.

Go Sell!

Before every call you make, review your notes and milestones and consider what this Buyer or Partner needs to experience to move the deal forward to the next milestone in their Ideal Buying Experience. Invest equal time in each buying experience milestone; don't just focus on prospecting or closing. Move all the deals in your pipeline forward at a steady pace, with two exceptions.

First, if you are near the end of a sales period and need to be sure you meet your quota, or have authorization to offer limited-time incentives to buyers, focus on deals that are likely to close before the end of the sales period. Second, if you have a clog in your sales pipeline with a massive number of deals sitting at the same milestone, consider the best way to move half those deals forward over the next week or two.

17

Week Three: Pursuing Profitable Partners

Now that you've established your Master List, segmented and prioritized, and created an Ideal Buying Experience for your Current Prospects, it's time to set up a regular cadence of new habits that will drive opportunities forward as efficiently as possible. With Profitable Routines, the purpose of efficiency is not just to get more done in less time, but to allow you to focus more time on strategic wins. Once you have fully adopted the Profitable Routine introduced this week, no high-potential sales deal will fall through the cracks on your watch.

Exercise One: Design an Ideal Buying Experience for Current Partners (30 minutes)

As you've established your Profitable Routines sales plan throughout this first month, new elements have been layered into your plan each week as you focus on immediate productivity and performance gains. Last week, you created an Ideal Buying Experience for your Current

Prospects. This week, you will use a similar method to create an Ideal Buying Experience for your Current Partners.

Take a few minutes now to review the names of your Current Partners in your Master List. Grab a blank sheet of paper, and list the five standard milestones for a buying experience:

∞ Engage

∞ Understand

∞ Educate

∞ Inspire

∞ Commit

Label the top of the page, "Ideal Buying Experience for Current Partners." Now, take a few minutes now to get into the hearts and minds of your Current Partners. Try to see yourself, your products and your company from their point of view. Consider their felt needs, hopes, and expectations when the phone rings, and they recognize your number. Or when you email them to set up a meeting to discuss your work together and set goals for the coming weeks or months.

Once again, set aside the administrative side of running transactions and focus on your partner's optimal interactions with you during a sale to one of their referrals. When you work with a partner, every action and conversation takes place in front of an audience, and that audience is the buyer, your partner's client. Consider that reality as you make notes on the specific steps, conversations, interactions, and turning points that you and the partner must work through together in order to move from initial introduction to closed sale. What are the bare basics you need to run a transaction with a partner? What does the partner need to hear, see, feel, or experience—distinct from what the buyer needs—in order to keep moving forward?

Remember that the single most important element in a partnership is trust. Build this sensitivity into your Ideal Buying Experience for Current Partners. Pay special *attention* to any step or stage that could feel risky to them. If you are thoughtful and proactive about this process, you can build trust and endear yourself to your partners, avoiding anything that could potentially embarrass them or cause them to feel you have cut them out of a deal.

Now document your thoughts in the form of a series of stages or milestones in the Ideal Buying Experience for your Current Partners. Finally, review the Current Partners in your Master List, and assign a milestone to each based on the new Buying Experience you just created.

Congratulations! You now have a clear, strategic plan to engage your Current Partners in their optimal buying process. This, along with your clear prioritization and understanding of what constitutes an ideal versus a tough partner, will help you to work more effectively with partners to find, pursue, and close more deals in the coming weeks.

Exercise Two: Next Actions (15 minutes)

In the final exercise this week, fully adopt your new core discipline: Next Actions. This single habit is shared by all the best salespeople in the world. Their collective mantra could be summed up as, "Every qualified prospect, lead, and opportunity must have a next step defined, with a due date." That's how the very best ensure good follow-up, solid prospecting, steady progress through the sales process, and a rich stream of referrals after a deal is closed. Every time you complete a Next Action with a prospect, immediately plan and schedule the very next Next Action. Make this a habit.

Your next task is simple: schedule a recurring weekly appointment to spend an hour reviewing every Active name in your Master List, and scheduling a Next Action for each of them. Easy, right? Good, time to get going. When the pre-scheduled hour comes to plan your Next Actions, focus relentlessly without distractions on this simple but critical discipline to keep your sales plan moving forward.

Go Sell!

This week, compare the amount of time and effort you dedicate to working with your current buyers and partners versus your future buyers and partners. Make deliberate and strategic decisions about how to shift that percentage, if necessary, to meet your immediate sales goals. Also, remember to update the "Active" tag for each name on your Master List as appropriate to reflect your shift in emphasis on future versus current buyers and partners.

18

Week Four: Establish your System

Exercise One: Design an Ideal Buying Experience for Current Customers (30 minutes)

Your next step in creating a sales strategy based on Profitable Routines is to consider how best to engage your Current Customers to find potential for new business. This is your third time designing an Ideal Buying Experience, so you're likely a pro at it now! Here again are the key steps in the process.

Envision a few of your best and favorite Current Customers, and begin to shift your point of view to empathize with theirs. On a blank sheet of paper, list the five standard stages for a buying experience:

- ∞ Engage

- ∞ Understand

- ∞ Educate

- ∞ Inspire

- ∞ Commit

Label the top of the page, "Ideal Buying Experience for Current Customers." What are the bare basics you need to engage a Current Customer in a new sales process?

What does the buyer need to hear, see, feel, or experience in order to respond positively throughout the process? List your needs and theirs, side by side, on a timeline. Group those tasks, needs, and expectations into a series of milestones in the Ideal Buying Experience for your Current Customers. Finally, review the Current Customers in your Master List, and note the stage that reflects their current status in the Buying Experience you just defined.

Exercise Two: Select and Pursue your Current Customers (30 minutes)

Review the Current Customers in your Master List, and update the "Active" prospect flag based on your work in the last exercise. Elevate those buyers you feel would respond positively to solicitation for new business, removing the Active designation for those you don't think would respond positively. Now, go sell.

Optional Exercise: Plan your Profitable Routines Month (15 minutes)

Having completed these exercises over the past month, you should have a sense of the immense backlog of untapped potential that exists today in your target market. At times, this backlog can be overwhelming. Remember, your goal with Profitable Routines is not to finish everything on your list, but rather to focus on the best things on your list. The key in the coming months will be to revisit these Profitable Routines weekly, or even daily. The time you invest in learning more about your target market and building your skills to better engage, influence, understand, and serve that market will pay rich dividends. It's worth your time to build a reputation as a competent Hunter and a responsible Farmer who has earned the love and respect of your target market.

Over the past month, you've focused on implementing Profitable Routines to deliver an immediate net gain in productivity and sales performance. For every hour you worked on your new sales plan, hopefully you've gained ten to twenty hours in improved focus on the best deals to pursue. You now have a clearer understanding of the needs of your buyers and partners, and better, more simplified tracking of your sales leads and prospects.

Your focus on immediate gains has provided:

- ∞   A first draft of your Master List of Buyers and Partners
- ∞   A clear definition of the Top Attributes of an Ideal/Tough Buyer
- ∞   A clear definition of the Top Attributes of an Ideal/Tough Partner
- ∞   An initial plan for the percentage of time you spend with prospects based on their assigned priorities
- ∞   An Ideal Buying Experience for your Current Prospects
- ∞   An Ideal Buying Experience for your Current Customers
- ∞   An Ideal Buying Experience for your Current Partners

Over the next month, you may also want to create an Ideal Buying Experience:

- ∞   To engage your Future Prospects
- ∞   To engage your Former Customers
- ∞   To engage your Former Partners

19

Creating Momentum

The sales world is a constant revolving door of relationships, as you relentlessly build and rebuild trust and rapport, month after month. Many times, it feels like you never get a day of rest—even when you feel stuck, tired, and overwhelmed. I'm sensitive to this. Profitable Routines is not about having to learn one more process, or creating more work for late nights and long weekends. Trust me, I've been in your shoes. Once you embrace Profitable Routines, it will reduce your stress, help you get in sync with your target market, and make every conversation, call, and follow up more focused and effective. I know the last thing you need on your plate is more work. So Profitable Routines is about making everything you do more effective; this is a compelling reason to change the strategies and habits that are in place today.

This system works. Period. It is worth your while to apply it to your day-to-day activities.

How many hours a week are you willing to dedicate to your Profitable Routines sales plan over the next ninety days?

Once you have completed the four-week plan to implement Profitable Routines, daily and weekly attention to this system will help you to maintain your new sales momentum. Think about it: continuing these simple habits is far simpler than letting go, getting behind, and then trying to catch up at the end of the quarter, right?

Action leads to movement. Movement leads to momentum. Momentum leads to achievement.

I challenge you to continue these new actions—they will lead you to success. Continue to revisit each routine from week to week, month after month. Continue to update your Master List and Priorities, reconsider your Ideal Buying Experience, Select and Pursue and plan Next Actions for every active prospect and sales opportunity.

I challenge you to focus the next ninety days on these basic sales activities. Use the Profitable Routines sales plan with steady, consistent effort. This is not a time to Shoot the Moon, Bag the Elephant, Beach the Whale, or pull a Hail Mary. Every sales strategy is difficult if you are inconsistent, and going for broke is just as inconsistent as laziness. Simply focus on the basics for three months. Plan your work, and work your plan.

Profitable Routines works best when you don't jump around. Focus on just one Profitable Routine each day, for at least twenty to sixty minutes. Then, take a break and go do something else. In other words, if you are in the midst of planning your Next Steps, don't make a phone call or answer emails. Just focus on planning your Next Steps. Trust the process, knowing that you will always have something to do at any time, with any energy level, to move your sales pipeline forward.

Each week, review and update your sales plan based on each of the five core disciplines of Profitable Routines. Update your Master List, Segment and Prioritize the names on the list, review and revise your Ideal Buying Experiences, Select and Pursue the best prospects each week, and diligently adopt the habit of Next Actions.

Success is not a lottery, it never comes from luck, and it always requires discipline. Over the past few weeks, you have shifted your sales behavior, adding new actions and rejecting others. These actions have likely already created new movement in your sales pipeline, as new relationships and business opportunities are beginning to appear. As you persist with these actions that are creating forward movement in your business, momentum will build. And momentum is a key ingredient in the alchemy we call success.

Every sale begins with your belief, with the moral compulsion that you have the power to improve someone's quality of life. From there, you continue through a series of tests that must prove not only the value of your product or service, but also your ability to plan a sales strategy to maximize every hour of every day you invest in growing your business. This is the proving ground of every salesperson. It is your daily habits, work patterns, and understanding of the sales environment that will ultimately allow you to excel.

I salute you for having the diligence, discipline, and commitment to your goals to truly engage and adopt Profitable Routines as a plan to help you sell. I look forward to hearing your success story soon.

Acknowledgments

Thanks to Elizabeth Marshall, Lynn Hare, Rebecca Shelley, Doris Leissing, Joyce Ferguson, Mike Caplan, Warren Thomas, Collin Andersen, Patrick Lewis, Jeff Aden, Tim Cowart, Larry Nordlinger, Pam Vredevelt, and Amy Rose Davis for their top-notch input, counsel, and encouragement.

A huge thanks to my mentors and colleagues, who taught me half of everything I know about business and consulting. And to my clients and competitors, who taught me the other half.

And to my amazing wife: I never have time enough with you, or words enough to say how much I love you.

About the Author

Christopher Bates is a sales and marketing consultant to Fortune 500 corporations, entrepreneurs, startups, and small- to mid-size businesses, and is a regular speaker at business seminars and guest lecturer for colleges and university MBA programs. Throughout his career, Christopher has helped thousands of business leaders grow their businesses profitably by showing them how to attain and retain more of the right kind of clients in their markets.

He has logged over 10,000 billable consulting hours across public and private sector organizations. He has spent the equivalent of over a hundred days transiting the troposphere to visit clients, befriended hundreds of taxi drivers, survived an attempted mugging, and made a lot of mistakes - most of which he never intends to repeat. He continues to speak to groups large and small, helping business leaders grow their market share by staying in sync with their target market.

In addition to his consulting work, Christopher has founded four companies of his own, and regularly assists with local and global community and economic development. He lives in the beautiful Pacific Northwest USA, where he writes, flies small airplanes, and hangs out with his wife and children and a great group of friends.

WORKSHOPS AND TRAINING

For information about Profitable Routines consulting workshops and training events for your organization, please visit www.profitableroutines.com.

INDEX

CHRISTOPHER BATES